Non-Native Fish Control below Glen Canyon Dam—Report from a Structured Decision-Making Project

By Michael C. Runge[1], Ellen Bean[1], David R. Smith[2], and Sonja Kokos[3]

Open-File Report 2011–1012

U.S. Department of the Interior
U.S. Geological Survey

[1] U.S. Geological Survey, Patuxent Wildlife Research Center, 12100 Beech Forest Rd., Laurel, MD 20708. mrunge@usgs.gov.
[2] U.S. Geological Survey, Leetown Science Center, 11649 Leetown Rd, Kearneysville, WV 25430.
[3] Bureau of Reclamation, Lower Colorado Region MSCP, Boulder City, NV 61470.

U.S. Department of the Interior
KEN SALAZAR, Secretary

U.S. Geological Survey
Marcia K. McNutt, Director

U.S. Geological Survey, Reston, Virginia: 2011

For more information on the USGS—the Federal source for science about the Earth,
its natural and living resources, natural hazards, and the environment,
visit http://www.usgs.gov or call 1–888–ASK–USGS.

For an overview of USGS information products, including maps, imagery, and publications,
visit http://www.usgs.gov/pubprod

To order this and other USGS information products, visit http://store.usgs.gov

Suggested citation:
Runge, M.C., Bean, Ellen, Smith, D.R., and Kokos, Sonja, 2011, Non-native fish control below Glen Canyon Dam—
Report from a structured decision-making project: U.S. Geological Survey Open-File Report 2011–1012, 74 p., at
http://pubs.usgs.gov/of/2011/1012/.

Contents

1. Abstract.. 1
2. Introduction 2
    2.1. Purpose... 4
    2.2. Legal and Regulatory Context.. 5
    2.3. Ecological Context 7
    2.4. Cultural Context 8
3. Decision Framework.. 8
4. Objectives 9
    4.1. Fundamental Objectives Hierarchy 12
    4.2. Measurable Attributes 13
    4.3. Narratives for Objectives and Attributes..15
5. Alternatives 23
    5.1. Action Elements 24
    5.2. Single Strategies 27
    5.3. Hybrid Portfolios...28
    5.4. Adaptive Strategies 32
6. Consequences of the Hybrid Strategies 33
    6.1. Methods 33
    6.2. Evaluation of Cultural Objectives 33
    6.3. Evaluation of Ecological Objectives 36
    6.4. Evaluation of Recreational Objectives..42
    6.5. Evaluation of Public Service Objectives 44
    6.6. Estimation of the Likelihood of the Assumptions 49
7. Decision Analysis 52
    7.1. Swing Weighting 52
    7.2. Analysis of Hybrid Portfolios in the Face of Uncertainty...54
    7.3. Value of Information 56
    7.4. Adaptive Strategies 59
8. Summary and Discussion..60
    8.1. Disagreement about the Science 60
    8.2. Cultural Values and the Viewpoint of the Tribes 61
    8.3. High-Flow Experimental Dam Releases (HFE) 62
    8.4. Linked Decisions...63
    8.5. Learning as a Means Objective...63
9. Acknowledgments 64
10. References Cited..65
Appendix 1 Letter from Anne Castle to Adaptive Management Working Group and Technical Working Group Members and Alternates, September 17, 2010 67
Appendix 2 Detailed Description of the Hybrid Portfolios...69
    Abbreviations Used...69
    Reference Cited 74

Figures

Figure 1. Location map of the Colorado River ecosystem below Glen Canyon Dam, depicting the Glen Canyon Dam Adaptive Management Program project area. 3
Figure 2. Hierarchy of fundamental objectives for non-native fish control below Glen Canyon Dam 10
Figure 3. Action elements for alternative control strategies for (A) removal of non-native fish, and (B) suppression of non-native fish or other non-removal actions designed to enhance humpback chub populations in the Colorado River below Glen Canyon Dam 25
Figure 4. Flowchart showing key uncertainties in predicting the response of rainbow trout and humpback chub populations to management actions 32
Figure 5. Conceptual model of fish community dynamics in the Colorado River below Glen Canyon Dam 38
Figure 6. Graph showing principal-components analysis of the objective weights 54
Figure 7. Flowchart showing the preferred alternatives as a function of the underlying hypotheses 57
Figure 8. Graph showing expected performance of three hybrid portfolios as a function of the weight on the rainbow trout (RBT) hypothesis 58

Tables

Table 1. Measurable attributes for the fundamental objectives 14
Table 2. Single strategies for removal or suppression of non-native fish, or enhancement of humpback chub populations in the Colorado River below Glen Canyon Dam 27
Table 3. Hybrid portfolios, composed of multiple single strategies (table 2), for removal or suppression of non-native fish, or enhancement of humpback chub populations 29
Table 4. Consequence matrix for cultural objectives 33
Table 5. Consequence matrix for ecological objectives 36
Table 6. Predictions of Lees Ferry rainbow trout recruitment and emigration to Marble Canyon as affected by flow policies, and incorporated into the model to predict consequences of alternatives on ecological objectives 40
Table 7. Predicted humpback chub response as a function of the combinations of three hypotheses 41
Table 8. Consequence matrix for recreational objectives 42
Table 9. Consequence matrix for economic and public service objectives 45
Table 10. Consequence matrix for strategic objectives 48
Table 11. Expert elicitation of the weight of evidence in favor of three underlying hypotheses 51
Table 12. Objective weights 53
Table 13. Composite scores from the multi-criteria decision analysis for each hybrid portfolio, using the objective and hypothesis weights of the individual agencies and Tribes 55
Table 14. Expected value of perfect information for discerning among the underlying hypotheses 56

Conversion Factors and Abbreviations

Inch/Pound to SI

Multiply	By	To obtain
Length		
inch (in.)	2.54	centimeter (cm)
inch (in.)	25.4	millimeter (mm)
foot (ft)	0.3048	meter (m)
mile (mi)	1.609	kilometer (km)
Flow rate		
cubic foot per second (ft^3/s)	0.02832	cubic meter per second (m^3/s)

Temperature in degrees Celsius (°C) may be converted to degrees Fahrenheit (°F) as follows:

$$°F=(1.8×°C)+32$$

Temperature in degrees Fahrenheit (°F) may be converted to degrees Celsius (°C) as follows:

$$°C=(°F-32)/1.8$$

Vertical coordinate information is referenced to the North American Vertical Datum of 1988 (NAVD 88). Horizontal coordinate information is referenced to the North American Datum of 1983 (NAD 83). Altitude, as used in this report, refers to distance above the vertical datum.

Abbreviations Used

AMWG	Adaptive Management Working Group
AZGF	Arizona Game and Fish Department
BIA	Bureau of Indian Affairs, Department of the Interior
BNT	Brown trout (*Salmo trutta*)
CRSP	Colorado River Storage Project
DOI	U.S. Department of the Interior
EA	Environmental Assessment
ESA	Endangered Species Act of 1973
EVPI	Expected value of perfect information
GCDAMP	Glen Canyon Dam Adaptive Management Program
GCMRC	Grand Canyon Monitoring & Research Center, U.S. Geological Survey
GCNP	Grand Canyon National Park, National Park Service
GCNRA	Glen Canyon National Recreation Area, National Park Service
GCPA	Grand Canyon Protection Act of 1992
HBC	Humpback chub (*Gila cypha*)
HFE	High-flow experiment
LCR	Little Colorado River
MLFF	Modified Low Fluctuating Flow
NEPA	National Environmental Protection Act
NHPA	National Historic Preservation Act of 1966
NPS	National Park Service, Department of the Interior
PBR	Paria to Badger reach, Colorado River
RBT	Rainbow trout (*Onchorhynchus mykiss*)
Reclamation	Bureau of Reclamation, Department of the Interior
RM	River mile (location along the Colorado River, relative to Lees Ferry)
ROD	1996 Record of Decision
SDM	Structured decision making
Service	U.S. Fish and Wildlife Service, Department of the Interior
USGS	U.S. Geological Survey, Department of the Interior
WAPA	Western Area Power Administration, Department of Energy

Non-Native Fish Control below Glen Canyon Dam— Report from a Structured Decision-Making Project

By Michael C. Runge[4], Ellen Bean[4], David R. Smith[5], and Sonja Kokos[6]

1. Abstract

This report describes the results of a structured decision-making project by the U.S. Geological Survey to provide substantive input to the Bureau of Reclamation (Reclamation) for use in the preparation of an Environmental Assessment concerning control of non-native fish below Glen Canyon Dam. A forum was created to allow the diverse cooperating agencies and Tribes to discuss, expand, and articulate their respective values; to develop and evaluate a broad set of potential control alternatives using the best available science; and to define individual preferences of each group on how to manage the inherent trade-offs in this non-native fish control problem.

This project consisted of two face-to-face workshops, held in Mesa, Arizona, October 18–20 and November 8–10, 2010. At the first workshop, a diverse set of objectives was discussed, which represented the range of concerns of those agencies and Tribes present. A set of non-native fish control alternatives ("hybrid portfolios") was also developed. Over the 2-week period between the two workshops, four assessment teams worked to evaluate the control alternatives against the array of objectives. At the second workshop, the results of the assessment teams were presented. Multi-criteria decision analysis methods were used to examine the trade-offs inherent in the problem, and allowed the participating agencies and Tribes to express their individual judgments about how those trade-offs should best be managed in Reclamation's selection of a preferred alternative.

A broad array of objectives was identified and defined, and an effort was made to understand how these objectives are likely to be achieved by a variety of strategies. In general, the objectives reflected desired future conditions over 30 years. A rich set of alternative approaches was developed, and the complex structure of those alternatives was documented. Multi-criteria decision analysis methods allowed the evaluation of those alternatives against the array of objectives, with the values of individual agencies and tribes deliberately preserved.

Trout removal strategies aimed at the Paria to Badger Rapid reach (PBR), with a variety of permutations in deference to cultural values, and with backup removal at the Little Colorado River reach (LCR) if necessary, were identified as top-ranking portfolios for all agencies and Tribes. These PBR/LCR removal portfolios outperformed LCR-only removal portfolios, for cultural reasons and for effectiveness—the probability of keeping the humpback chub population above a desired threshold was estimated to be higher under the PBR/LCR portfolios than the LCR-only portfolios. The PBR/LCR removal portfolios also outperformed portfolios based on flow manipulations, primarily because of the

---

[4] U.S. Geological Survey, Patuxent Wildlife Research Center, 12100 Beech Forest Rd., Laurel, MD 20708. mrunge@usgs.gov.
[5] U.S. Geological Survey, Leetown Science Center, 11649 Leetown Rd, Kearneysville, WV 25430.
[6] Bureau of Reclamation, Lower Colorado Region MSCP, Boulder City, NV 61470.

effect of sport fishery and wilderness recreation objectives, as well as cultural objectives. The preference for the PBR/LCR removal portfolios was quite robust to variation in the objective weights and to uncertainty about the underlying dynamics, at least over the ranges of uncertainty investigated.

Examination of the effect of uncertainty on the recommended outcomes allowed us to complete a "value of information" analysis. The results of this analysis led to an adaptive strategy that includes three possible long-term management actions (no action; LCR removal; or PBR removal) and seeks to reduce uncertainty about the following two issues: the degree to which rainbow trout limit chub populations, and the effectiveness of PBR removal to reduce trout emigration downstream into Marble and eastern Grand Canyons, where the largest population of humpback chub exist. In the face of uncertainty about the effectiveness of PBR removal, a case might be made for including flow manipulations in an adaptive strategy, but formal analysis of this case was not conducted.

The full set of conclusions described above is not definitive, however. This analysis described in this report is a simplified depiction of the true decision; it is only meant to aid decision-makers by helping them see the structure of the problem, not to make the decision for them. This analysis can best be used as a starting point for the deliberative consultations that will lead to the final decision. In particular, this structured decision-making process will be useful to the Department of the Interior (DOI) as it undertakes an analysis of removal strategies under the National Environmental Policy Act.

2. Introduction

The Glen Canyon Dam is located on the Colorado River in Arizona, USA, upstream of Grand Canyon National Park (fig. 1), and is managed by the Bureau of Reclamation (Reclamation). The Glen Canyon Dam Adaptive Management Program (GCDAMP) was established in 1997 to provide input to Reclamation and the DOI on the effects to the downstream ecosystem resulting from operation of the dam. The GCDAMP project area stretches along the Colorado River from the forebay of Glen Canyon Dam to the westernmost boundary of Grand Canyon National Park (this area is henceforth referred to as "the Canyon"). Locations along the river are indexed by river miles (RM), with a reference point at Lees Ferry (RM 0). The dam itself is at RM −15.5 (15.5 mi upstream of Lees Ferry). Other important locations that are referenced in this report include the following: Paria River (RM 1.0), Badger River (RM 8.0), Little Colorado River (RM 61.4), and Bright Angel Creek (RM 87.8). The reach from Lees Ferry to the Little Colorado River is known as Marble Canyon; Grand Canyon proper begins at the Little Colorado River.

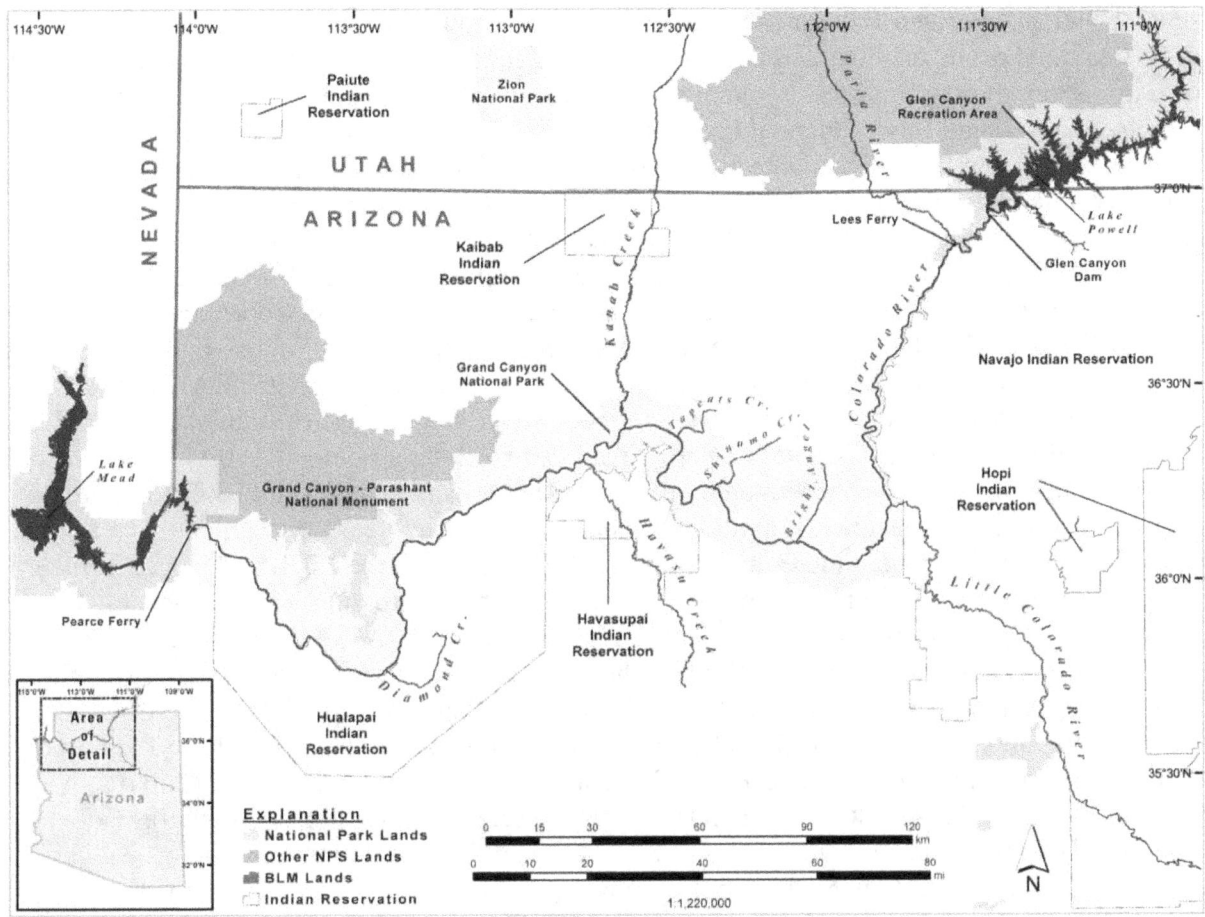

Figure 1. Location map of the Colorado River ecosystem below Glen Canyon Dam, depicting the Glen Canyon Dam Adaptive Management Program project area. The analysis described in this report focuses primarily on the Colorado River from Glen Canyon Dam to Bright Angel Creek. Map credit: Thomas Gushue, U.S. Geological Survey.

In the 2008 Biological Opinion on Reclamation's proposed experimental dam operations for Glen Canyon Dam, the U.S. Fish and Wildlife Service (Service) found that the actions may affect humpback chub (*Gila cypha*), an endangered fish, and Kanab ambersnail (*Oxyloma haydeni kanabensis*), an endangered land snail. As part of this Biological Opinion, the Service included non-native fish control as a conservation measure, to address the threat to humpback chub posed by rainbow trout (*Onchorhynchus mykiss*) and brown trout (*Salmo trutta*). Mechanical removal of trout at the confluence of the Colorado River and Little Colorado River (LCR) was experimentally implemented in 2003–06, and was shown to be effective at controlling trout populations (Coggins, 2008; Coggins and Yard, 2010; Coggins and Yard, in press). An increase in humpback chub adult abundance was observed over the same period of time, but the causal connection is in dispute. In accordance with the 2008 Biological Opinion, one additional mechanical removal trip in the LCR treatment reach occurred in spring 2009.

Several Native American Tribes raised serious concerns about the lethal removal of thousands of fish from the treatment reach, an area sacred to the Tribes and fundamental to their religious beliefs and ceremonies. In response to this concern, Reclamation decided to forego planned mechanical removal in 2010 and initiated a National Environmental Protection Act (NEPA) process that would use an Environmental Assessment (EA) to evaluate alternative methods for non-native fish control.

There are a number of cooperating agencies and Tribes interested in this EA process. Reclamation is responsible for operation of Glen Canyon Dam and is the decision-making agency for this non-native fish control EA. The Service is responsible for administering the Endangered Species Act (ESA), including recovery of the humpback chub; and the Fish and Wildlife Coordination Act for conservation of fish and wildlife resources. The National Park Service (NPS) administers both the Grand Canyon National Park (GCNP) and the Glen Canyon National Recreation Area (GCNRA), and is responsible for trust resources and public recreation in those areas. The Bureau of Indian Affairs (BIA) has a trust responsibility to the Tribes. The Western Area Power Administration (WAPA) is responsible for marketing and delivery of power generated by the dam. The Arizona Game and Fish Department (AZGF) regulates sport fishing statewide, including rainbow trout in the Lees Ferry tailwaters reach and rainbow and brown trout throughout the Canyon. For the Pueblo of Zuni, the LCR, and its confluence with the Colorado River, are sacred places and tied to their accounts of creation. The non-beneficial destruction of life is of grave concern to them. For the Hopi Tribe, the entire Grand Canyon and especially the LCR are deeply sacred areas. Further, they agreed, when they emerged into this world, to be caretakers of the Canyon. Lands of the Navajo Nation and the Hualapai Tribe border the Colorado River, with the reservations of the two Kaibab Bands of Paiute Indians nearby. All of these Tribes have an interest in the management of resources. The U.S. Geological Survey (USGS) Grand Canyon Monitoring and Research Center (GCMRC) is responsible for scientific investigations that provide information to the GCDAMP about the status of key resources of the river below the dam, as well as ecosystem modeling that serves to help guide monitoring and experimental design decisions.

The problems related to non-native fish control are multi-faceted and complex. One problem is the many competing objectives within and among agencies and Tribes. Other problems are that all the management options have not been clearly defined and the ecological science about the effects of potential management alternatives on the natural resources is uncertain. Also there is uncertainty about the effects of potential management alternatives on cultural resources.

The Assistant Secretary of the Interior for Water and Science, in a letter to the Adaptive Management Working Group dated September 17, 2010, asked that Reclamation undertake a Structured Decision Making (SDM) process to evaluate options for non-native fish control, as an additional means by which the cooperating agencies and Tribes could submit their input to Reclamation as it prepares its EA (appendix 1).

2.1. Purpose

The purpose of this report is to describe a structured approach developed by the U.S. Geological Surevey (USGS), to develop and provide substantive input to Reclamation for use in preparation of an EA concerning management of non-native fish below Glen Canyon Dam. The structured approach provided a forum for the diverse cooperating agencies and Tribes to discuss, expand, and express their respective values; to develop and evaluate a broad set of potential non-native fish control alternatives using the best available science; and to indicate how they would individually prefer to manage the inherent trade-offs in this resource management problem.

This structured approach has two important facets: it promotes value-focused thinking, that is, an emphasis on the values that underlie a decision; and it uses problem decomposition to disentangle the complicated scientific and policy elements of a decision. The intended methods for this structured approach include multi-criteria decision analysis (Hammond and others, 1999), an approach for understanding how decision alternatives affect the achievement of an array of multiple objectives.

Two workshops were held in Mesa, Arizona prior to release of the draft EA for public comment. At the first workshop, objectives were defined and alternative fish control strategies (called "portfolios" throughout this report) created. Between the first and second workshops, four assessment teams evaluated the portfolios against the individual objectives. At the second workshop, representatives from the agencies and tribes weighted objectives, and a preliminary analysis of the decision was completed. This preliminary analysis led to insights about objectives, alternatives, and consequences; as a result, a number of modifications to the analysis were requested. A consolidated list of alternatives was carried forward in the final analysis.

2.2. Legal and Regulatory Context

Reclamation proposes to control non-native fish in the Colorado River downstream of Glen Canyon Dam to ensure that its operations do not jeopardize the continued existence of endangered native species. Since passage of the ESA and its implementing regulations (50 CFR 402), Reclamation has consulted with the Service to ensure that its operation of Glen Canyon Dam does not jeopardize the continued existence of the endangered endemic Colorado River fishes—humpback chub and razorback sucker (*Xyrauchen texanus*)—or destroy or adversely modify their designated critical habitat. Colorado pikeminnow (*Ptychocheilus lucius*) and bonytail chub (*Gila elegans*) are no longer found in this reach of the Colorado River and are not included in this assessment. One of six populations of humpback chub occurs in the GCDAMP project area (fig. 1) and the razorback sucker occurs immediately downstream of the project area.

Critical habitat for these fishes was designated by the Service in 1994 (50 CFR 17) and includes areas in Marble and Grand Canyons. For humpback chub, critical habitat extends for 175 mi of the Colorado River from Nautiloid Canyon (RM 34) to Granite Park (RM 209) and the lower 8 mi of the LCR. Critical habitat for razorback sucker extends for 234 mi of the Colorado River from the Paria River confluence (RM 1) to the Lake Mead inflow at maximum pool (RM 235). These reaches of designated critical habitat lie within the boundaries of GCNRA and GCNP and are managed by NPS.

Reclamation and the Service have agreed that controlling the numbers of non-native fish would serve as a conservation measure for Reclamation's dam operations. Non-native fish control was identified as a conservation measure in the February 27, 2008, Final Biological Opinion on the Operation of Glen Canyon Dam (U.S. Fish and Wildlife Service, 2008, consultation number 22410-1993-F-167R1), and the October 29, 2009, Supplement to the 2008 Final Biological Opinion for the Operation of Glen Canyon Dam (U.S. Fish and Wildlife Service, 2009, consultation number 22410-1993-F-167R1). Control of non-native fish species in Marble and Grand Canyons is also part of the conservation measures identified in the 2007 Biological Opinion for the Proposed Adoption of Colorado River Interim Guidelines for Lower Basin Shortages and Coordinated Operation for Lake Powell and Lake Mead (U.S. Fish and Wildlife Service, 2007, consultation number 22410-2006-F-0224). A fourth biological opinion on the cancellation of nonnative mechanical removal trips in 2010 was issued on November 9, 2010 (U.S. Fish and Wildlife Service, 2010, consultation number 22410-1993-F-167R2), and required as a term and condition that Reclamation

"Resume nonnative control at the mouth of the LCR in 2011. Attempt to implement the program in a manner compatible with the interests of Tribes and other interested stakeholders.

"AND/OR

"Work with interested Tribes and other parties, expeditiously, to develop options that would move nonnative removal outside of LCR confluence tribal sacred areas in 2011, with the goal that nonnative removal of trout in sacred areas will be reserved for use only to ensure the upper incidental take level is not exceeded."

Once Reclamation accepted these conservation measures, implementation of non-native fish control became a part of proposed action, although there is discretion in exactly where, when, and how non-native fish control is conducted.

Reclamation is serving as the lead Federal agency in this action because it has operational authority over Glen Canyon Dam and it has agreed to the terms of the biological opinions issued by the Service. Reclamation's implementation of additional non-native control measures during 2011–12 (and potentially additional periods) will be analyzed through the ongoing NEPA process and subsequent further ESA consultation. However, Reclamation's legal authority does not include direct management of Colorado River fishes. Agencies with such authority include AZGF, the state resource agency responsible for managing sport fish; NPS, the Federal land management agency responsible for the multitude of resources within GCNRA and GCNP; and the Service, under the ESA. In the biological opinions to Reclamation, these control actions need to be coordinated with other agencies, such as the Service, AZGF, and NPS, because of their responsibilities for managing aquatic and fishery resources in the Glen, Marble, and Grand Canyons.

Laws that govern Reclamation's actions and convey some of the values of the people of the United States as they pertain to ecological and cultural resources are numerous. The following paragraphs include a partial list of those laws.

The ESA of 1973, as amended (16 USC 1531 *et seq.*), requires that all U.S. Federal agencies shall seek to conserve threatened and endangered species, and utilize their authorities in furtherance of the purposes of the ESA. Action agencies must implement Section 7 consultations with the Service to ensure that "…any action authorized, funded, or carried out by such an agency…is not likely to jeopardize the continued existence of any endangered or threatened species or result in the destruction or adverse modification of habitat of such species."

The National Historic Preservation Act of 1966, as amended (NHPA, 16 USC 470 *et seq.*), requires Federal agencies to take into account the effects of their undertakings on historic properties. Historic properties are those that are included in, or eligible for inclusion in, the National Register of Historic Places. The NHPA makes specific provisions for inclusion of places of religious and cultural significance to Native American Tribes on the National Register.

The Grand Canyon Protection Act of 1992 (GCPA, Pub. L. 102–575, title XVIII) requires the Secretary of Interior to operate Glen Canyon Dam "…in accordance with the additional criteria and operating plans specified in section 1804 and exercise other authorities under existing law in such a manner as to protect, mitigate adverse impacts to, and improve the values for which GCNP and GCNRA were established, including, but not limited to natural and cultural resources and visitor use."

As part of its ongoing implementation of the GCDAMP, which serves to implement obligations established by the GCPA, in late 2010 Reclamation was in the process of developing an EA for a high-flow experimental release protocol (separate from the non-native fish control EA), the purpose of which is to improve the natural resources of the Canyon through sandbar-building flows.

2.3. Ecological Context

Two goals of the Glen Canyon Dam Adaptive Management Working Group (AMWG) are to conserve endangered aquatic species, and to preserve native communities and ecological processes within the Colorado River. Ensuring the persistence of humpback chub is a core component of this mission, and requires a dual purpose research program to better understand humpback chub ecology and threats to the species persistence.

The presence of non-native fish is an acknowledged primary threat to native fish, and two introduced predatory species, rainbow trout and brown trout, are of particular concern. These species also may have indirect negative effects on humpback chub persistence by competing for resources and habitat. Dietary research (Yard and others, in press; Coggins and Yard, 2010) demonstrates that non-native trout prey upon humpback chub, with brown trout displaying higher rates of predation than rainbow trout. However, the potential benefit of reduced predation by rainbow trout is attenuated given the abundance of that species below the dam in Grand Canyon National Park (Makinster and others, 2010). Whereas preliminary evidence indicates that predation is an important limiting factor, the full extent to which trout limit humpback chub population growth and affect age-structure is unknown.

Beginning in January 2003, and continuing through August 2006, in response to a recommendation by the AMWG, Reclamation initiated an experimental research program to examine the potential effect on humpback chub recovery of reducing the population size of non-native fish. The site of the removal, the confluence of the LCR with the main stem of the Colorado River (fig. 1), is an important spawning and rearing area for humpback chub and other native species. All captured non-native fish were removed from the system. Results of the removal experiment are detailed in Coggins (2008), Coggins and Yard (2010), and Coggins and others (in press), but two key findings are relevant to the decision analysis, particularly to the impact of uncertainty on the decision process. Trout removals may have been effective in altering community level dynamics and in causing a simultaneous increase in native abundance along with juvenile survival and recruitment. The results are inconclusive, however, owing to a concurrent natural increase in river-wide temperatures resulting from drought in the Upper Colorado River Basin and decreased storage in Lake Powell that benefitted native fish ecology, and a system-wide decrease in rainbow trout abundance, possibly linked to changes in the aquatic food base. Another important factor that confounded the removal experiment is the high degree to which naturally occurring turbidity varies in the main channel in response to infrequent, but large tributary flooding from the Paria River (RM 1).

Whereas the results of the removal trials may have demonstrated a clear, direct link between trout abundance and humpback chub population persistence, further experimentation would be needed to tease apart other system level dynamics that could have contributed to adult humpback chub population increases observed since 2000 (Coggins and Walters, 2009). The predictive models used to assess consequences of the proposed portfolios incorporate this uncertainty. Other key areas of uncertainty considered relate to the effects of artificial floods released from the dam (high flow experiments intended to rebuild and maintain sandbars) on rainbow trout spawning; recruitment and adult population growth (Korman and others, 2010; Korman and others, in press; Makinster and others, 2010); and the efficacy of manipulating flow regimes to reduce trout survival and downstream emigration into Marble and Grand Canyons.

2.4. Cultural Context

The motivation for broadening the scope of the discussion of non-native fish control is to address concerns expressed by members of the AMWG, specifically its Tribal partners. Through formal and informal consultation, some Tribes have indicated that current practices that result in the massive taking of life present an unnecessary emotional, psychological, and spiritual burden on their communities.

As described by the Governor of Zuni,

"the Grand Canyon figures as an extremely important place in the history, religion and culture of the Zuni people. The Grand Canyon is a vital component of the Zuni cultural landscape that contributes to the definition of who we are as a people."

This sentiment has also been expressed by other participating Tribes, and highlights the profound relationship with, and deep respect for, the landscape that includes the Colorado River and its tributaries. Because of this relationship, some Tribes possess a strong sense of stewardship for the life found within the Canyon, including both native and non-native fish species. Large-scale lethal removal, especially in the face of perceived uncertainty regarding the effects of non-native fish on native fish, is a violation of this stewardship ethic.

Further, the location of the prescribed removal is primarily at the confluence of the LCR with the mainstem of the Colorado River, a place of great power and life-sustaining properties for many Tribal partners. Actions taken here, especially if coupled with lethal or otherwise disrespectful methods, can result in a disruption of the balance and interconnectedness within the universe.

3. Decision Framework

Reclamation's Upper Colorado River Regional office is the sole decision-maker for this EA. Several agencies and Tribes are formal Cooperating Agencies for this EA (BIA, Service, NPS, WAPA, AZGD, GCMRC, Pueblo of Zuni, and Hualapai Tribe), and several additional Tribes have a strong vested interest (Hopi Tribe, Southern Paiute Consortium, and Navajo Nation). The decision analysis developed at these SDM workshops, and described in this report, is meant to allow the Cooperating Agencies and Tribes to provide substantive input to Reclamation as it considers its decision about a preferred alternative for non-native fish control below Glen Canyon Dam. This future action is being considered particularly in order to reduce the threat posed by non-native fish to humpback chub. The methods ultimately employed need to be within the jurisdiction of Reclamation.

Reclamation desires to release a draft EA to the public in January 2011, with consultation under section 7 of the ESA and a decision notice to be completed by March 1, 2011. The time frame of the actions proposed in the EA will be on the order of 5 years, but there is some recognition that the strategy employed may have longevity beyond that time. DOI is also in the process of conducting government-to-government tribal consultation on this action.

The decision in the EA is a one-time decision and a single preferred alternative needs to be identified and implemented for the period of time specified. But there is strong recognition that the preferred alternative may have state-dependent features in which certain components of the strategy may only be implemented if and when certain conditions are met. Further, the preferred alternative may also be adaptive, in that a range of strategies may need to be experimentally tested, to reduce uncertainty about the most effective strategies.

Thus, the decision problem can be characterized as one of multiple-objective trade-offs in the face of uncertainty, where the management actions are multi-faceted and possibly state-dependent, and where there may also be opportunities to reduce uncertainty early and improve management later through adaptive implementation.

4. Objectives

Defining values that affect a decision is an important first step in decision analysis. A commonly understood and comprehensive vision about the underlying values to guide future steps was an important first step for this project. This includes defining a set of standards that could be used to measure progress for each objective.

The first SDM workshop provided a structured framework for listening to all voices and incorporating each stakeholder's values into the decision process. Taken together, the objectives represent a range of values and perspectives that apply to the control of non-native fish in the lower Colorado River. For Federal and State agencies, these values arise from their respective missions, enabling legislation, regulatory responsibilities, and constituent concerns. For the Tribes, the values arise more directly from their cultural and spiritual traditions. The combined set of values provides, in part, the necessary guidance for making an informed and defensible choice of a preferred alternative for non-native fish control and underscores the aspects of the decision that matter.

Four main categories of decision-making objectives were identified (Keeney, 2007). *Fundamental objectives* are sometimes described as the "bottom line," or core concern, and can be identified when the question of "why is this important" concludes with "simply because" or "it just is". *Means objectives* are often methodological and describe an intermediary step in reaching a fundamental objective, in other words they address the "how." Means objectives are not important in and of themselves, but only insofar as they help achieve the fundamental objectives. *Process objectives* describe the ground rules for the decision process itself. For example, within the context of this workshop, we established open and consultative communication as an objective that would be adhered to throughout. Similarly, any proposed objectives or actions would need to comply with the large regulatory framework under which all the cooperating agencies and Tribes operate. *Strategic objectives* are objectives that are fundamental to a broader set of decisions than the one in question; they cannot be solely attained by the decision at hand, but there can be a contribution to them. Often strategic objectives are tied to linked decisions and broader mandates of the decision makers.

The focus of this section of the report is on the fundamental objectives, as these make explicit the key concerns of the lead and cooperating agencies as well as the Tribal groups. Although certain stakeholder groups (for example, sport fisheries and recreational user groups) were not formally represented within the official cooperating partners, their concerns were included by soliciting information from knowledgeable agency partners (especially, AZGF and NPS). Plenary and small group formats were implemented to discuss and craft the set of objectives. Through a deliberative process, the group worked to distinguish between the various types of objectives, as well as to eliminate redundant objectives and to consolidate similarly defined objectives.

Four broad classes of fundamental objectives were identified after much discussion. These classes summarize (1) the cultural and spiritual dimensions of the non-native fish control issue, (2) ecological aspects including both species and ecosystem level components, (3) recreational interests and uses, and (4) operational and economic components of the issue (fig. 2). A fifth class of objectives was identified between the two workshops; these are strategic objectives that concern the authority, jurisdiction, and legal responsibilities of Reclamation. In the analysis, these objectives will not be traded-off against other objectives, rather, they will serve to screen for admissible non-native fish control alternatives.

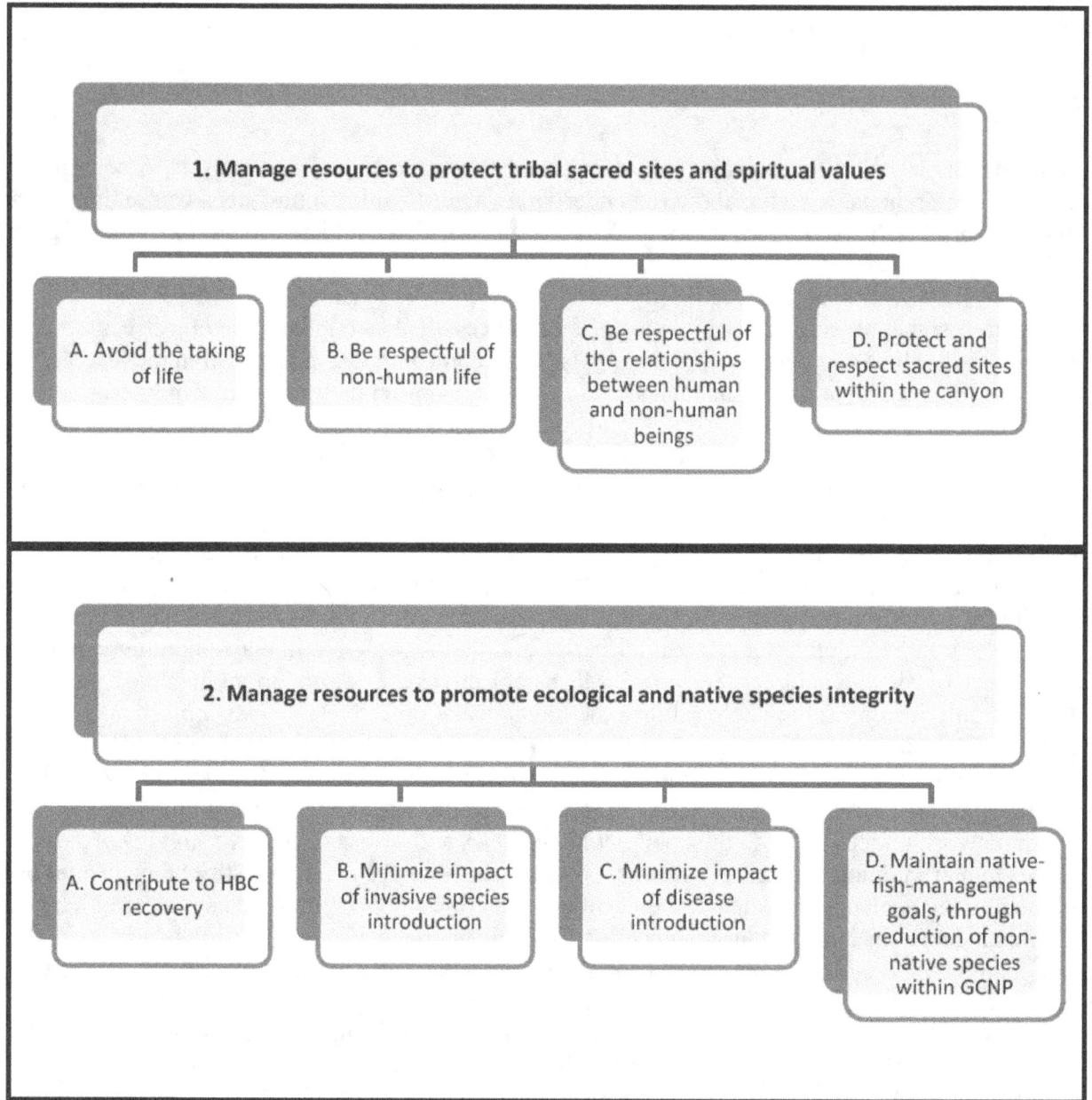

Figure 2. Hierarchy of fundamental objectives for non-native fish control below Glen Canyon Dam. HBC, humpback chub; GCNP, Grand Canyon National Park; GCNRA, Glen Canyon National Recreation Area; Reclamation, Bureau of Reclamation; HFE, high-flow experiment; NHPA, National Historic Preservation Act.

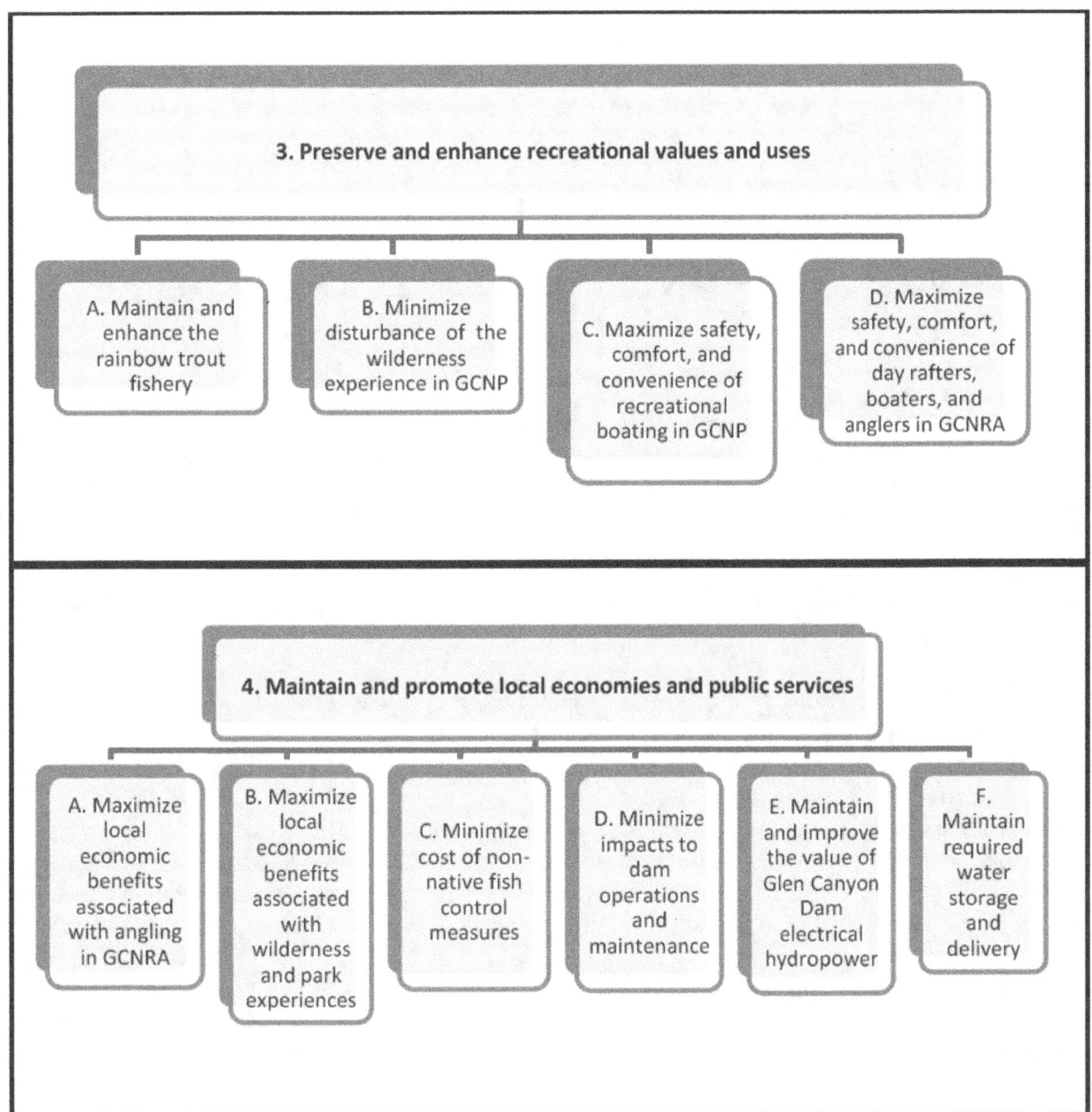

Figure 2. Hierarchy of fundamental objectives for non-native fish control below Glen Canyon Dam.—Continued

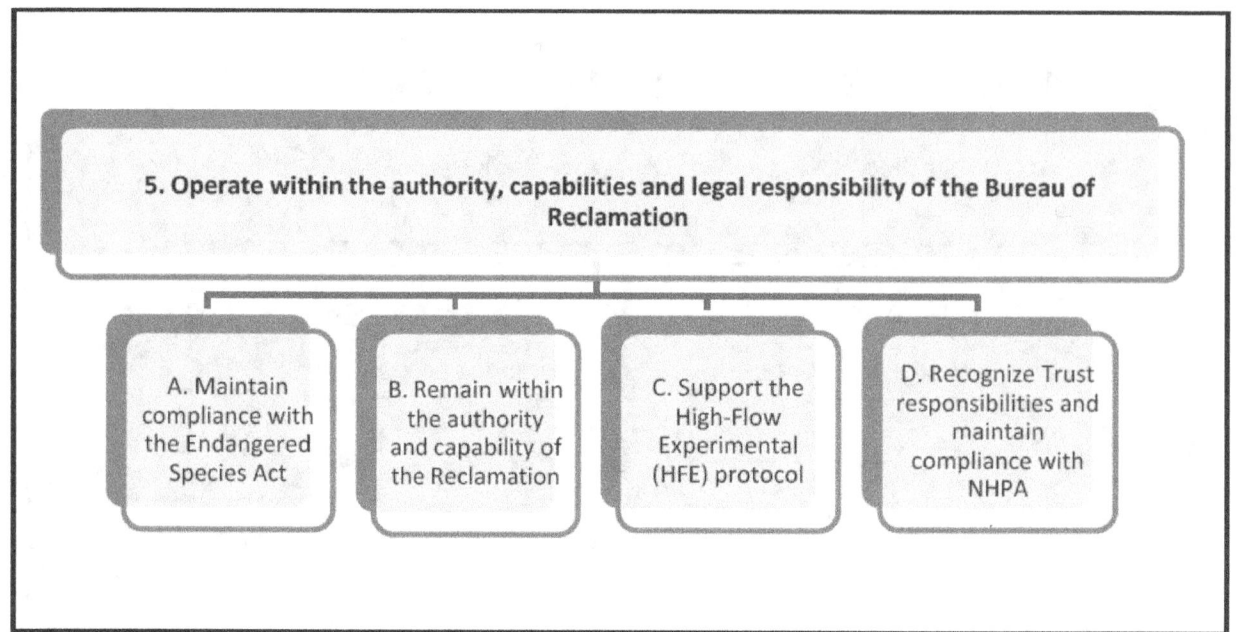

Figure 2. Hierarchy of fundamental objectives for non-native fish control below Glen Canyon Dam.—Continued

With particular reference to the Tribal cooperating partners, each Tribe has a distinct voice and perspective, and the proposed objectives and attributes may not fully reflect either the nuances within, or diversity among, the Tribes. The full spectrum of concerns within a Tribe may not have been addressed with these objectives, and will require further consultation with community members and elected leaders. As of late 2010, DOI is in the process of conducting government-to-government tribal consultation on this action, but this is not yet complete. The Hualapai Tribe had limited involvement in this process owing to other engagements, and representatives from both the Southern Paiute Consortium and Navajo Nation were unable to attend for the full duration of both workshops. This process and this report, therefore, do not represent definitive statements of the objectives of the Tribes, merely an attempt to identify the main features that are important.

4.1. Fundamental Objectives Hierarchy

The draft set of fundamental objectives is shown in the hierarchy below (and also in fig. 2). Detailed descriptions of each of the objectives are found in Section 4.3. Note that the order of presentation of the fundamental objectives is not meant to imply an order of preference.

1. Manage resources to protect tribal sacred sites and spiritual values
    A. Avoid the taking of life
    B. Be respectful of non-human life
    C. Be respectful of the relationships between human and non-human beings
    D. Protect and respect sacred sites within the Canyon

2. Manage resources to promote ecological and native species integrity
   A. Contribute to humpback chub recovery
   B. Minimize impact of invasive species introduction (including risk of introduction, impact of spread, and opportunities for mitigation and treatment)
   C. Minimize impact of disease introduction (including risk of introduction, impact of spread, and opportunities for mitigation and treatment)
   D. Maintain native-fish-management goals, through reduction of non-native species within Grand Canyon National Park

3. Preserve and enhance recreational values and uses
   A. Maintain and enhance the rainbow trout fishery within the Lees Ferry tailwaters reach (RM –16 to RM 0) to provide a memorable experience for anglers
   B. Minimize disturbance of the wilderness experience as a result of non-native fish management in the wilderness-managed area of GCNP
   C. Maximize safety, comfort, and convenience of recreational boating in the wilderness-managed area of GCNP, as affected by flow regimes from Glen Canyon Dam
   D. Maximize safety, comfort, and convenience of day-rafters, boaters, and anglers in the GCNRA, as affect by flow regimes from Glen Canyon Dam

4. Maintain and promote local economies and public services
   A. Maximize local economic benefits associated with angling in GCNRA (Lees Ferry tailwaters reach)
   B. Maximize local economic benefits associated with wilderness and park experiences
   C. Minimize cost of non-native fish control measures
   D. Minimize impacts to dam operations and maintenance
   E. Maintain and improve the value of Glen Canyon Dam electrical hydropower
   F. Maintain required water storage and delivery to downstream users

5. Operate within the authority, capabilities, and legal responsibility of the Bureau of Reclamation
   A. Maintain compliance with the Endangered Species Act
   B. Remain within the authority and capability of Reclamation
   C. Support the High-Flow Experimental (HFE) protocol
   D. Recognize Trust responsibilities and maintain compliance with section 106 of the NHPA

4.2. Measurable Attributes

Measurable attributes are scales on which fundamental objectives can be evaluated. These are sometimes also called performance measures. Measurable attributes evaluate how well a particular alternative is likely to achieve the aspirations expressed by each objective. The measurable attributes are shown in table 1, and described more fully in Section 4.3.

Table 1. Measurable attributes for the fundamental objectives.

[HBC, humpback chub; LCR, Little Colorado River; GCNP, Grand Canyon National Park; RBT, rainbow trout; GCNRA, Glen Canyon National Recreation Area; ESA, Endangered Species Act of 1973; NHPA, National Historic Preservation Act of 1966; $/yr, dollars per year]

Fundamental objective	Measurable attribute
1. Manage resources to protect tribal sacred sites and spiritual values	
A. Avoid the taking life	1A. Yes/No, life taken
B. Be respectful of non-human life	1B. Relative respectfulness of use, scale 1–10
C. Be respectful of the relationships between human and non-human beings	1C. Yes/No, culturally appropriate
D. Protect and respect sacred sites within the Canyon	1D. Yes/No, interferes with sanctity of the canyon
2. Manage resources to promote ecological and native species integrity	
A. Contribute to humpback chub recovery	2A. Probability of HBC adult abundance at LCR greater than 6,000 over the next 30 years
B. Minimize impact of invasive species introduction (including risk of introduction, impact of spread, and opportunities for mitigation and treatment)	2B1. Likelihood of introduction to Glen or Grand Canyon: none, low, medium, high 2B2. Likelihood of introduction from Glen or Grand Canyon: none, low, medium, high
C. Minimize impact of disease introduction (including risk of introduction, impact of spread, and opportunities for mitigation and treatment)	2C1. Likelihood of introduction to Glen or Grand Canyon: none, low, medium, high 2C2. Likelihood of introduction from Glen or Grand Canyon: none, low, medium, high
D. Maintain native-fish-management goals, through reduction of non-native species within GCNP	2D1. RBT abundance within GCNP 2D2. Frequency of HBC adult abundance greater than 10,000 over the next 30 years
3. Preserve and enhance recreational values and uses	
A. Maintain and enhance the rainbow trout fishery within the Lees Ferry tailwaters reach to provide a memorable experience for anglers	3A1. Catch rate (fish/hr) 3A2. Fraction of trout greater than 20 in.
B. Minimize disturbance of the wilderness experience as a result of non-native fish management in the wilderness-managed area of GCNP	3B. Penalized user-days
C. Maximize safety, comfort, and convenience of recreational boating in the wilderness-managed area of GCNP, as affected by flow regimes from Glen Canyon Dam	3C. Days/year that flow is within specifications
D. Maximize safety, comfort, and convenience of day-rafters, boaters, and anglers in the GCNRA, as affected by flow regimes from Glen Canyon Dam	3D. Days/year that flow is within specifications

Fundamental objective	Measurable attribute
4. Maintain and promote local economies and public services	
A. Maximize local economic benefits associated with angling in GCNRA (Lees Ferry tailwaters reach)	4A. Annual economic value ($)
B. Maximize local economic benefits associated with wilderness and park experiences	4B. Annual economic value ($)
C. Minimize cost of non-native fish control measures	4C. Total cost of action ($)
D. Minimize impacts to dam operations and maintenance	4D. Yes/No, compatibility with schedule
E. Maintain and improve the value of Glen Canyon Dam electrical hydropower	4E. Relative economic value ($/yr)
F. Maintain required water storage and delivery to downstream users	4F. Yes/No, compatibility with specified responsibilities
5. Operate within the authority, capabilities, and legal responsibility of the Bureau of Reclamation	
A. Maintain compliance with the ESA	5A. Relative efficacy of method, scale 0–2
B. Remain within the authority and capability of Reclamation	5B. Yes/No, with commentary
C. Support the High-Flow Experimental Protocol	5C. Yes/No, provide robust non-native fish options in the face of flow effects
D. Recognize Trust responsibilities and maintain compliance with section 106 of the NHPA	5D. Three-point constructed scale

4.3. Narratives for Objectives and Attributes

Where not otherwise noted, the objectives were developed to reflect long-term desired conditions, where "long-term" was interpreted as being 30 years or more.

Objective 1A. *Avoid the taking of life.* This reflects, in part, the belief in the sanctity of life and the role that aquatic life plays in traditional belief systems and creation stories of the participating Tribal nations. The taking of life is non-trivial and the relative acceptability of its occurrence is entirely dependent upon the respect paid in its taking and its purposeful use. Within the context of the decision problem at hand, the legitimacy and acceptability of the taking of non-native fish life depends upon the benefits to the humpback chub population, and the final use of the trout lethally removed from the ecosystem.

Measurable attribute 1A: Utility scale (0-1), where a score of 0 indicates that life is taken under the hybrid portfolio, and a score of 1 indicates that it is not.

Objective 1B. *Be respectful of non-human life.* This reflects a stewardship ethic, and states that the taking of life should be purposeful and only done with good intent, and that in its taking, other life should be sustained.

Measureable attribute 1B: The 10-point constructed scale considers the relative degree of respectfulness for the proposed end uses, with a score of 0 indicating a strong lack of respect and a score of 10 indicating a strong respect for the lives of the fish taken. The value may differ among the Tribes and other stakeholders.

Objective 1C. *Be respectful of the relationships between human and non-human beings.* This objective reflects a world view recognizing that human and non-human lives are inter-connected and that no living being is superior to another. Any action taken that affects one life form may have ripple effects that radiate out and affect other life forms. Because of this, human interactions with the world must minimize the disturbance and potential cause of harm, by being respectful of these relationships. Otherwise, these interactions may lead to the loss of balance between living beings. This philosophy serves as a foundation for traditional practices by the Tribes.

Measurable attribute 1C: Utility scale (0-1), where a score of 0 indicates that the method of capture is not culturally appropriate, and a score of 1 indicates that it is culturally appropriate. Intermediate values reflect the degree of appropriateness.

Objective 1D. *Protect and respect sacred sites within the Canyon.* This objective reflects the importance of the Canyon in the traditional cultures, beliefs, and practices of the Tribes. Disturbance to the Canyon, and to sites of historical and spiritual significance specifically, leads to the degradation of the sanctity of the Canyon. This degradation in turn leads to the further alienation of Tribal communities from the Canyon, and interferes with their ability to fulfill their role in maintaining ecological, cultural, and social harmony within the world.

Measurable attribute 1D: Utility scale (0-1), where a score of 0 indicates the hybrid portfolio negatively affects the sanctity of the Canyon and a score of 1 indicates the portfolio protects and respects the sanctity of the Canyon. Intermediate values reflect the degree of protection of the sanctity of the Canyon.

Objective 2A. *Contribute to humpback chub recovery.* According to the Biological Opinion for the Operation of Glen Canyon Dam (February 27, 2008), Reclamation is a primary contributor to the development of the GCDAMP Comprehensive Plan for the management and conservation of humpback chub in Grand Canyon, and continues to work with GCDAMP cooperators to develop a comprehensive approach to management of humpback chub. Dam-controlled flow has the potential to affect humpback chub directly or indirectly through effects on predator or competitor species abundances. Non-native rainbow and brown trout, among other non-native fishes, are potential predators and competitors of humpback chub and Reclamation has proposed measures to achieve conservation benefits for humpback chub. The Service has used adult humpback chub abundance in recent biological opinions on Glen Canyon Dam operations to gauge the efficacy of these measures against the adverse effects of dam operations.

Measurable attribute 2A: Probability of the adult humpback chub population remaining above 6,000 over the next 30 years. Adult humpback chub in the LCR remaining above a threshold (6,000) abundance over 30-years has been proposed as an attribute that links to population viability and humpback chub population status. This attribute was predicted using a Population Viability Analysis (PVA) model, and abundance has been estimated and monitored using an age-structured mark recapture model (Coggins, 2007; Coggins and Walters, 2009).

Objective 2B. *Minimize impact of invasive species introduction (including risk of introduction, impact of spread, and opportunities for mitigation and treatment).* Introduction of invasive species can have far reaching impacts on native species, impacts which are difficult or impossible to reverse. Opportunities for mitigation or treatment depend on early detection of introductions, and preventing introduction could be the most efficient approach to invasive species management. Several species are of primary concern at present. The New Zealand mudsnail (*Potamopyrgus antipodarum*) currently inhabits the Colorado River primarily in Glen Canyon (Cross and others, 2010). Prevalence is high and distribution is throughout Glen and Grand Canyons. Trout consume mudsnails but they may pass through their digestive system unaffected. Movement of live trout from Glen or Grand Canyons to other receiving waters would be a likely vector for introduction to unaffected waters. There is some evidence that *Didymosphena geminata* (didymo or rock snot) occurs in Glen and perhaps Grand Canyon. Prevalence is low or suspect. Transport of water (with live trout) to other watersheds could be a vector for introduction of didymo to unaffected waters or watersheds. Invasive species could be introduced to Glen or Grand Canyon through stocking of trout at Lees Ferry.

> Measurable attribute 2B1: Likelihood of introduction of invasive species to Glen or Grand Canyon. This attribute is a 4-point constructed scale to measure the risk of impact. The attribute has two components: (1) prevalence of invasive species and (2) frequency of vector events. Each component ranges numerically from 3 (high prevalence or frequency) to 0 (no prevalence or frequency). The component scores are assessed and multiplied, and then the product is converted to the 4-point scale of none, low, medium, or high.

> Measurable attribute 2B2: Likelihood of translocating invasive species from Glen or Grand Canyon to an outside location. This attribute is a 4-point constructed scale to measure the risk of impact. The attribute has two components: (1) prevalence of invasive species and (2) frequency of vector events. Each component ranges numerically from 3 (high prevalence or frequency) to 0 (no prevalence or frequency). The component scores are assessed and multiplied, and then the product is converted to the 4-point scale of none, low, medium, or high.

Objective 2C. *Minimize impact of disease introduction (including risk of introduction, impact of spread, and opportunities for mitigation and treatment).* Introduction of disease to fish populations can reduce productivity or lead to extirpation. Treatment options can be costly, impractical, or unavailable. Preventing introduction of disease agents and controlling their spread is a basic management principle among natural resource agencies. Several diseases are of concern in Glen and Grand Canyons. Disease agents could be introduced to Glen or Grand Canyon through stocking of trout at Lees Ferry. The trout in Glen and Grand Canyon are considered exposed to Whirling Disease, a virulent salmonid disease detected in one lot of fish tested from Glen Canyon in 2003. Rainbow trout in Glen Canyon have not, however, displayed symptoms of the disease. Prevalence is considered low. Transport of live trout, or trout carcasses, to other receiving locations could result in introductions to unaffected waters and watersheds. The trout in Glen and presumably Grand Canyon carry an intestinal nematode that, under conditions of stress, can proliferate and affect the condition of individuals and populations. Transport of live trout, or trout carcasses, to other receiving locations could be a vector for introductions to unaffected waters and watersheds. Native fishes in Grand Canyon carry an intestinal parasite (Asian tapeworm), which is readily spread to other fishes. Asian tapeworm is relatively broadly distributed across Arizona. Transport of the parasite via this vector can be controlled through treatment, although the treatment is complicated and carries some risk to the fish.

Measurable attribute 2C1: Likelihood of introducing disease to Glen or Grand Canyon. This attribute is a 4-point constructed scale to measure the risk of impact. The attribute has two components: prevalence of disease and frequency of vector events. Each component ranges numerically from 3 (high prevalence or frequency) to 0 (no prevalence or frequency). The component scores are assessed and multiplied, and then the product is converted to the 4-point scale of none, low, medium, or high.

Measurable attribute 2C2: Likelihood of transporting disease from Glen or Grand Canyon to an outside location. This attribute is a 4-point constructed scale to measure the risk of impact. The attribute has two components: prevalence of disease and frequency of vector events. Each component ranges numerically from 3 (high prevalence or frequency) to 0 (no prevalence or frequency). The component scores are assessed and multiplied, and then the product is converted to the 4-point scale of none, low, medium, or high.

Objective 2D. *Maintain native-fish-management goals, through reduction of non-native species within GCNP.* According to NPS Management Policies (National Park Service, 2006), the NPS will maintain, as parts of the natural ecosystems of parks, all plants and animals native to park ecosystems. The NPS will act to preserve and restore the natural abundances, diversities, dynamics, distributions, habitats, and behaviors of native plant and animal populations and the communities and ecosystems in which they occur. Furthermore, the NPS will remove, when possible, or otherwise contain, individuals or populations of introduced or non-native species that have already become established in parks. High priority will be given to managing exotic species that have, or potentially could have, a substantial impact on park resources, and that can reasonably be expected to be successfully controlled. The NPS will survey for, protect, and strive to recover all species native to national park system units that are listed under the ESA.

Measurable attribute 2D1: Rainbow and brown trout abundance within GCNP. These attributes measure the level of non-native fish that could substantially impact the endangered humpback chub and other native fish. Abundance can be estimated through monitoring programs. Predicted abundance of rainbow trout in the LCR can be used as a proxy in decision analyses.

Measurable attribute 2D2: Frequency at which the adult humpback chub population in the LCR confluence reach remains above threshold abundance (10,000). Different from Measurable Attribute 2A, this attribute measures how often the annual population crosses this higher threshold (10,000), and has been proposed to measure how well proposed actions maintain NPS management goals for the endangered humpback chub.

Objective 3A. *Maintain and enhance the rainbow trout fishery within the Lees Ferry tailwaters reach (RM –16 to RM 0) to provide a memorable experience for anglers.* At one time, when the tailwaters provided a better food base, the Lees Ferry fishery was a national trophy rainbow trout fishery. Currently (2010), the fishery provides a unique angling experience in a desert tailwater environment; and this fishery could be enhanced to once again provide a high-quality, destination fishing experience that is respected nationally and attracts both national and international visitors. Two important aspects of the trout stock that would affect this experience are abundance and size-distribution. A larger population size results in a higher catch rate. When the size-distribution contains a high fraction of "preferred" fish (greater than 20 in.), anglers have more opportunity to catch large fish.

Measurable attribute 3A1: Catch rate (fish/hour), as measured by creel surveys. In 2009, the catch rate was 0.85 fish/hour (fish/hr), less than three-quarters of what it was in the late 1990s. The desire is to see this returned to the levels of the late 1990s (1.2 fish/hr). The catch rate predicted as part of this attribute should be the expected catch rate in the longer term (approximately 10 years) after the stock has adjusted to the new management conditions.

Measureable attribute 3A2: Fraction of the trout stock that is of at least "preferred" size (greater than 20 in.), as measured by electrofishing surveys. Currently, the stock is dominated by fish in the 6–8 in. range, with less than 0.5 percent greater than 20 in. The desire is to see this fraction increased to several percent, providing a non-negligible opportunity for anglers to catch a large fish. As with attribute 3A1, the predicted attribute should be the expected size-distribution in the long term after the stock has adjusted to the new management conditions.

Objective 3B. *Minimize disturbance of the wilderness experience as a result of non-native fish management in the wilderness-managed area of GCNP.* An important part of the recreational experience enjoyed by visitors to GCNP is the opportunity to be in a wilderness setting with minimal contact with other people and few sights and sounds associated with human activities. Non-native fish control activities, whether on foot, by boat, or by helicopter, and any infrastructure associated with them, however temporary, have the potential to undermine the wilderness experience for others (particularly people rafting the river or backpacking at river camping areas) and may be inconsistent with NPS wilderness policy. Effects of fish-control activities include the noise and lights associated with removal actions (especially when at night), the competition for camping sites along the river, and the simple presence of more people on the river.

Measurable attribute 3B: Penalized user-days per year in the GCNP wilderness during administrative trips for the purpose of non-native fish management. The staff size times the number of days in the wilderness is the basic measure; this is multiplied by a penalty factor for activities that result in greater disturbance. Penalty factor for boat (motor) user-days during motor season is 1; boat (motor) user-days during non-motor season, 2; helicopter trips, 2; and nighttime management activities, 3. Thus, for example, a 14-day removal trip with a staff of eight, conducted by boat during the non-motor season, with management activities primary at night would have a score of 672 penalized user-days (14 days × 8 users × 2 [non-motor] × 3 [night]). If helicopter removal of live fish was required, with 2 trips daily for 8 of the 14 days, an additional 32 penalized user-days (2 trips/day × 8 days × 2 [helicopter penalty]) would be added. The number of boats is not included in the calculation; presumably the number of users is tied to the number of boats.

Objective 3C. *Maximize safety, comfort, and convenience of recreational boating in the wilderness-managed area of GCNP, as affected by flow regimes from Glen Canyon Dam.* Several aspects of the flow regime from the dam can affect the experience of boaters in the Canyon. Low flows (under 8,000 cubic feet per second [ft^3/s]) can make a number of sections of the river dangerous or even possibly unnavigable. High flows (greater than 31,000 ft^3/s) can create uncomfortable or dangerous whitewater boating conditions in some places. Flows that fluctuate widely, particularly over a short period of time, can create unpredictable conditions for boating, and inconvenient conditions for camping. Current operating rules under the 1996 Record of Decision (ROD; U.S. Department of the Interior, 1996) specify maximum daily flow fluctuation ranges of 5,000, 6,000, or 8,000 ft^3/s (depending on the monthly release volumes). Daytime fluctuating flow operations are limited to between 8,000 and 25,000 ft^3/s under these daily operating rules, with hourly ramping rates restricted to 4,000 ft³/s per hour as flows increase and no greater than 1,500 ft³/s per hour as flows are ramped down following daily peaks. Daily lows can go to 5,000 ft³/s, but only between the hours of 07:00 pm and 07:00 am,

> Measurable attribute 3C: Number of days per year during which the flow from the dam operates inside of the following conditions that promote safety, comfort, and convenience for rafting in the wilderness area of GCNP—flows greater than 8,000 ft³/s, flows less than 31,000 ft³/s, daily fluctuations less than 5,000 ft³/s.

Objective 3D. *Maximize safety, comfort, and convenience of day-rafters, boaters, and anglers in the GCNRA, as affected by flow regimes from Glen Canyon Dam.* Several aspects of the flow regime from the dam can affect the experience of anglers, boaters, and rafters in the GCNRA. Extremely low flows (under 3,000 ft³/s) can make a number of sections of the Lees Ferry tailwaters reach unnavigable, particularly past 3-mile Bar (RM –3). High flows (greater than 30,000 ft³/s) can create uncomfortable or dangerous conditions in some places. Flows that fluctuate widely, particularly high upramping rates, can create unpredictable conditions for boaters and anglers.

> Measurable attribute 3D: Number of days per year during which the flow from the dam operates inside of the following conditions that promote safety, comfort, and convenience for angling and boating in GCNRA—flows greater than 3,000 ft³/s, and flows less than 30,000 ft³/s. Specific maximum upramp rates are not included because none of the alternative strategies had upramp rates outside of the 1996 ROD conditions. If faster upramp rates than the 1996 ROD conditions were considered, these rates might need to be included in this attribute.

Objective 4A. *Maximize local economic benefits associated with angling in GCNRA (Lees Ferry tailwaters reach).* The rainbow trout fishery provides economic and social benefit to a small rural community and to the region. A number of businesses (lodges, restaurants, guides, outfitters, and others) and individuals derive their income from anglers who come to Marble Canyon for the fishing experience. Whereas this economic benefit is associated with the number of angler-days, some factors (like the increase in day trips from larger cities) do not result in as much local economic benefit.

> Measurable attribute 4A: Annual economic value, in dollars, of the Lees Ferry tailwaters reach fishery to the local community. The predicted attribute should be the expected economic value in the long-term (approximately 10 years), after adjustments to the fishery and local economy owing to changes associated with new management conditions. We assume that the annual economic value is proportional to angler-days, with a multiplier of $210 per angler-day, on the basis of studies from Arizona State University (Silberman, 2003).

Objective 4B. *Maximize local economic benefits associated with wilderness and park experiences.* GCNP provides benefits to both local and regional economies. With regard to non-native fish management, the businesses that could be affected are those associated with wilderness recreation that originates at Lees Ferry, namely, white-water rafting. While the potential management actions being considered for non-native fish management could affect the experience of wilderness recreation, the demand for such opportunities is so high, and the supply so low, that it is unlikely that any of the potential actions will have a differential effect on this objective. Thus, while this objective is important, it does not help to distinguish any of the non-native fish control alternatives being considered.

Measurable attribute 4B: Annual economic value, in dollars, of the wilderness industry to the local economy. The predicted attribute should be the expected economic value in the long-term (approximately 10 years), after adjustments to the local economy because of changes associated with new management conditions. No effort was made to estimate this economic value, because it likely will not differ across the alternatives being considered.

Objective 4C. *Minimize cost of non-native fish control measures.* The GCDAMP and Reclamation have limited annual budgets. In the past, non-native control efforts have utilized flows from Glen Canyon Dam as well as electrofishing at the confluence of the Colorado and Little Colorado Rivers to limit numbers of non-native fishes, particularly rainbow and brown trout. Non-native fish control utilizing electrofishing to remove fish, predominantly the two trout species, has cost on average $150,000 per mechanical removal river trip, which includes logistics and research analysis. The costs of other strategies for removing non-native fish or reducing their survival and recruitment, as well as possible mitigation measures to offset tribal concerns, such as translocating live fish further downstream within GCNP or to other waters, need to be determined. This cost analysis does not take into consideration the costs to other resources, such as recreation, hydropower, or other monitoring and research needs of the GCDAMP, only the logistics and research associated with conducting non-native fish control activities.

Measurable attribute 4C: Cost in US Dollars, incorporating both fixed and variable costs over the next 5 years.

Objective 4D. *Minimize impacts to dam operations and maintenance.* Glen Canyon Dam has eight generating units, penstocks, and associated infrastructure. At any given time these units may be down for maintenance. Typically only one unit will be down, but at times up to three may be down. The dam also has requirements for regulation and spinning reserve that effectively reduce the release capacity by approximately 2,500–3,500 ft^3/s so that regulation and spinning reserves can be maintained. The maintenance schedule can be modified to meet certain release requirements or objectives, to some degree. This objective attempts to assess the degree to which different non-native fish control strategies may interfere with operation and maintenance of Glen Canyon Dam.

Measurable attribute 4D: Binary response (yes/no): operation is compatible with the maintenance schedule.

Objective 4E. *Maintain and improve the value of Glen Canyon Dam electrical hydropower.* Electricity is an integral part of every aspect of residential, commercial, and industrial life. The electricity produced at the dam is a renewable and environmentally preferred resource. The Glen Canyon Dam is integrated into the electrical production of several large Colorado River Storage Dams and it serves part of the needs of over 5 million people, in the rural Rocky Mountain and desert Southwest. The Dam provides a significant portion of the electrical needs of more than 50 Native American areas. Electricity is sold as a long-term firm product, at the cost of production, under terms that allow flexibility so as to schedule electrical power deliveries to maximize the value of the Glen Canyon Dam power resource.

Measurable attribute 4E: Annual economic value in dollars per year ($/yr) of power produced at Glen Canyon Dam, relative to current conditions.

Objective 4F. *Maintain required water storage and delivery to downstream users.* Glen Canyon Dam is operated by Reclamation and is the key water storage unit of the Colorado River Storage Project (CRSP). The CRSP and the Colorado River are managed and operated under numerous compacts, federal laws, court decisions and decrees, contracts, and regulatory guidelines collectively known as the "Law of the River." This collection of documents apportions the water and regulates the use and management of the Colorado River among the seven basin states and Mexico. Glen Canyon Dam is also operated to be in compliance with Treaty and Compact Delivery requirements under the 2007 Colorado River Interim Guidelines for Lower Basin Shortages and Coordinated Operations for Lake Powell and Lake Mead (Interim Guidelines), as well as the GCPA. This objective attempts to assess the degree to which different non-native fish control strategies may interfere with water storage and delivery operations of Glen Canyon Dam.

> Measurable attribute 4F: Binary response (yes/no): Operation is compatible with Reclamation's responsibilities for water storage and delivery.

Objective 5A. *Maintain compliance with the ESA.* The need for non-native fish control resulted from an ESA section 7 consultation on dam operations, and mechanical removal remains one of the recommended conservation measures in the operating biological opinion. Reclamation, as a Federal agency, has a responsibility to comply with Federal law, including the ESA. To a large degree, compliance with the ESA is reflected in the status of humpback chub (Objective 2A). However, one major aspect of ESA compliance is satisfaction of conservation measures. The current conservation measure calls for mechanical removal of trout at the mouth of the LCR. To evaluate whether an alternative would be equivalent to the mechanical removal conservation measure, one mode of analysis is to compare the effectiveness of various non-native control techniques with the effectiveness of mechanical removal as stated in the conservation measure.

> Measurable attribute 5A: 3-point constructed scale: action does not perform as well as original conservation measure (score: 0 points); action performs as well as original conservation measure (1 point); action outperforms original conservation measure (2 points); the performance of the action is unknown (n/a). This will be evaluated by Reclamation, and should be understood as Reclamation's perception of the likelihood of compliance, given past opinions and current information. This scale is not, of course, binding to the Service in subsequent biological opinions under section 7 of the ESA.

Objective 5B. *Remain within the authority and capability of Reclamation.* Reclamation has limited authority and limited capability in terms of the types of actions it can initiate, fund, or execute. Admissible alternatives will need to be within these bounds, and also within the scope of the Non-native Fish Control EA.

> Measurable attribute 5B: Binary scale (yes/no), with notes. If the alternative is within the authority and capability of Reclamation, and within the scope of the EA, it should be scored "yes." If not, it should be scored "no", with additional commentary on which agencies, Tribes, or other stakeholders have, perhaps joint, authority for the alternative.

Objective 5C. *Support the High-Flow Experimental Protocol.* In a separate ongoing EA process, Reclamation is considering alternatives for ongoing high-flow experimental releases from Glen Canyon Dam for the purposes of sandbar building in the Canyon. High-flow experimental releases have been one mechanism that DOI has historically used to comply with the GCPA. High flow releases are also believed to increase rainbow trout populations, perhaps depending on the time of year, and thus, may increase the threat to humpback chub through competition and predation. Non-native fish control alternatives that are not effective at robustly controlling trout and preventing jeopardy to humpback chub may undermine ongoing dam operations and could inhibit future dam operations such as high flow experiments that may increase the non-native fish population in the Canyon. This is largely related to whether the alternative will be compliant with the ESA (Objective 5A), but there may be other nuances to it.

> Measurable attribute 5C: Binary scale (yes/no): Does the alternative provide robust options for controlling rainbow trout, in the event that high-flow releases increase rainbow trout populations and the trout populations in turn negatively affect humpback chub?

Objective 5D. *Recognize Trust responsibilities and maintain compliance with section 106 of the NHPA.* The Federal government holds trust responsibilities that recognize the sovereign status and management authority of Tribes, and that assure the Tribes that Federal agencies will not knowingly compromise traditional practice and livelihoods in execution of their duties. Executive Order 13007 adds specificity to this principal in stating that Federal agencies "shall avoid adversely affecting the physical integrity of sacred sites," whereas Secretarial Order 3206 stipulates that within the context of the ESA the "Departments will carry out their responsibilities under the Act in a manner that harmonizes the Federal trust responsibility to tribes." Further, the NHPA requires Federal agencies to take into account the effects of their actions on historic properties, which, through the National Register includes special provisions for places of cultural and religious significance. To some degree, the cultural values outlined by Objectives 1A–1D reflect existing policy but those objectives do not clearly specify, nor fully encapsulate, the unique and complex relationship between the Tribes and the Canyon, a relationship that is recognized legally by the U.S. Claims Court and programmatically in the Strategic Plan adopted by the GCDAMP. The inclusion of this objective ensures that proposed alternatives support Federal responsibilities.

> Measurable attribute 5D: 3-point constructed scale: action does not perform as well as original conservation measure (score: 0 point); action performs as well as original conservation measure (1 point); action outperforms original conservation measure (2 points); the performance of the action is unknown (n/a). This will be evaluated by Tribal representatives, and should be understood as the Tribal perception of the likelihood of meeting those responsibilities, given past opinions and current information. This scale is not, of course, binding to Reclamation.

5. Alternatives

The non-native fish control alternatives under consideration are complex, multi-faceted approaches, which perhaps will involve adaptive components. To understand the structure of these alternatives, we built them up from the simplest components and identified several layers of complexity. At the simplest level, the alternatives consist of *action elements*, specific and detailed aspects of on-the-ground actions. Action elements that are related can be combined into *single strategies*, which focus on a particular method for addressing some aspect of the problem. The single strategies themselves can be combined into *hybrid portfolios*. These hybrid portfolios are meant to be the alternatives for long-term management of the resources, and are the focus of the evaluation (see section 6). In the short-term, however, because the hybrid portfolios are based on untested assumptions, consideration of *adaptive strategies* that include multiple hybrid portfolios may be warranted. Development and evaluation of potential adaptive strategies follows the initial evaluation of the hybrid portfolios.

5.1. Action Elements

Action elements in this problem fall into broad categories of (1) removal of non-native fish, (2) suppression of non-native fish, and (3) enhancement of humpback chub populations. Because each action element contains several options, the elements in this problem are complex (fig. 3). For example, options for removal of non-native fish include which species and age class to remove, magnitude of the removal, removal method, location and timing of the removal, and disposition of removed fish (fig. 3A). Also, there are several options for suppressing non-native fish or enhancing humpback chub populations that involve flow alterations, sediment augmentation (Randle and others, 2007), and other non-removal approaches (fig. 3B).

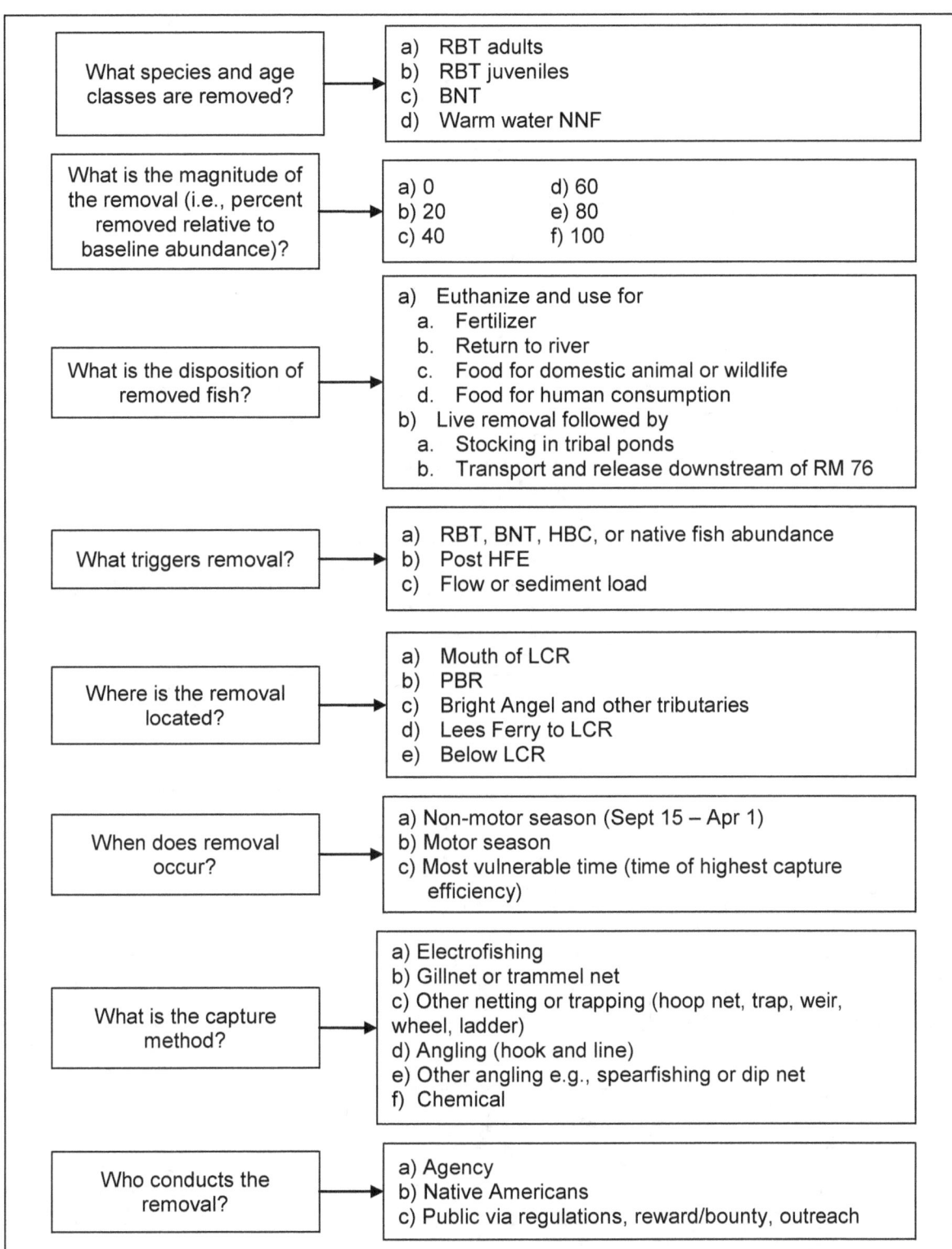

Figure 3. Action elements for alternative control strategies for (A) removal of non-native fish, and (B) suppression of non-native fish or other non-removal actions designed to enhance humpback chub populations in the Colorado River below Glen Canyon Dam.

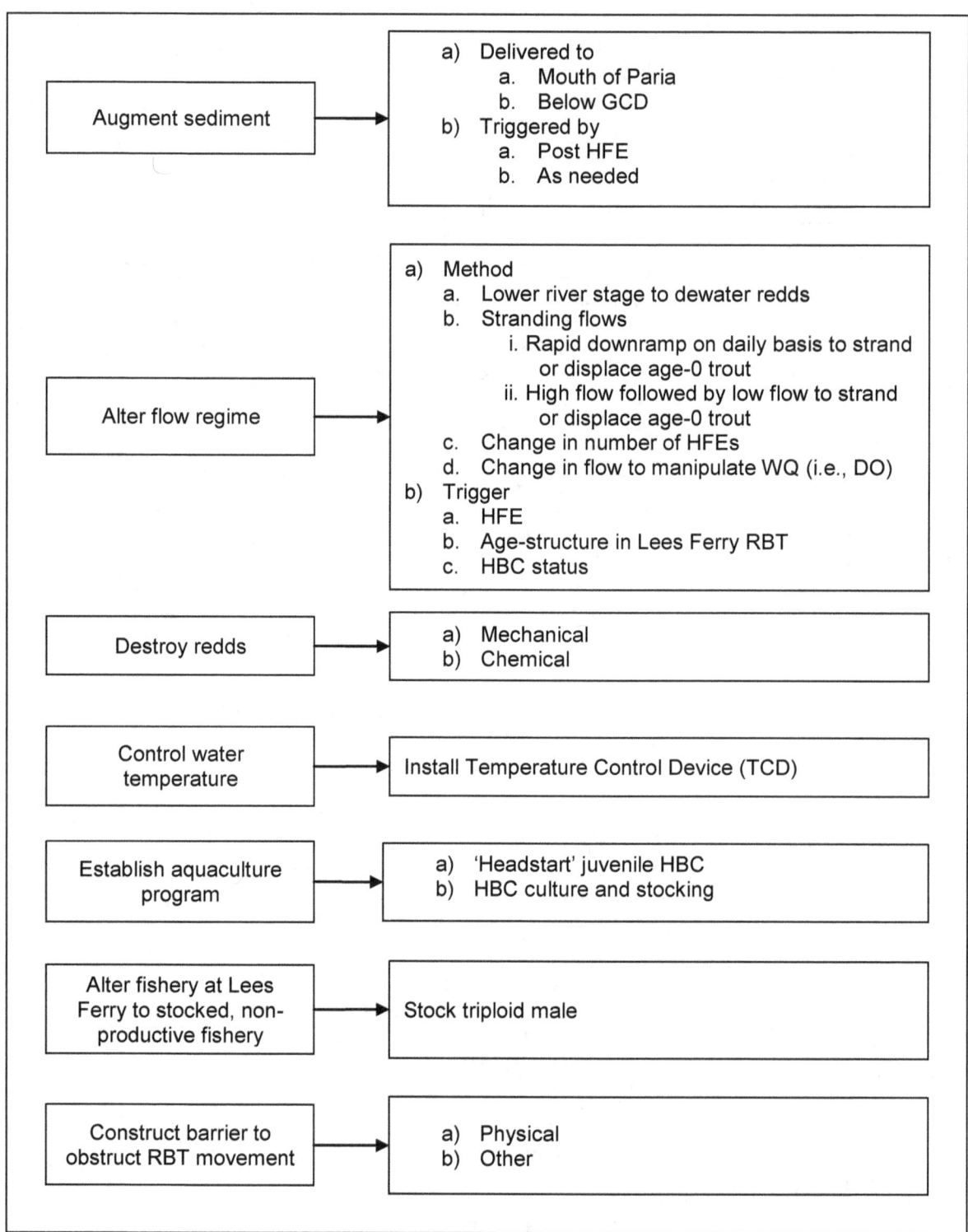

Figure 3. Action elements for alternative control strategies for (A) removal of non-native fish, and (B) suppression of non-native fish or other non-removal actions designed to enhance humpback chub populations in the Colorado River below Glen Canyon Dam.—Continued

5.2. Single Strategies

Action elements can be combined to form single strategies (table 2). These single strategies are meant to be precise descriptions of certain activities that might be undertaken, although it's not envisioned that any of these would be undertaken alone. Rather, the single strategies are building blocks for the hybrid portfolios. The single strategies range from no action with regard to rainbow trout (strategy 1) to the historical mechanical removal method (strategy 2) to stranding flows (strategies 9 and 11), sediment augmentation (strategies 13 and 14), and humpback chub headstarting (strategy 18). At this time, it is not yet clear which of these single strategies are within the jurisdiction of Reclamation and the scope of the non-native fish control EA, but this wide range is being explored to encourage a creative search for solutions.

Table 2. Single strategies for removal or suppression of non-native fish, or enhancement of humpback chub populations in the Colorado River below Glen Canyon Dam.

[RBT, rainbow trout; BNT, brown trout, LCR, Little Colorado River; PBR, Paria-to-Badger reach; HFE, High-flow experiment; ROD, Record of Decision; HBC, humpback chub]

1. No action with regard to RBT (action may or may not be taken with regard to BNT)
2. Lethal removal of RBT @ LCR, fertilizer use, 2–6 trips per year during the motor season as needed, 4–6 depletion passes per trip
3. Removal of adult RBT @ LCR, beneficial use (live or lethal), trout trigger (greater than 1,200 trout at LCR), up to 6 trips per year (Jan–Mar, Jul–Sep), 6 depletion passes per trip
    a. Electrofishing, euthanasia, freeze or smoke, human consumption
    b. Electrofishing, euthanasia, freeze, domestic or endangered animal consumption
    c. Gill netting, euthanasia, freeze or smoke, human consumption
    d. Gill netting, euthanasia, freeze, domestic or endangered animal consumption
    e. Electrofishing, live removal, stock tribal fish ponds
    f. Electrofishing, live removal, transport downstream (RM 76)
    g. Gill netting, live removal, stock tribal fish ponds
    h. Gill netting, live removal, transport downstream (RM 76)
    i. *And other possible options and combinations*
4. Removal of RBT adults 1.5 mi upstream from LCR confluence, beneficial use (live or lethal), RBT & HBC triggers (options the same as in #3 above)
5. RBT removal @ PBR, beneficial use (live or lethal), untriggered, 10 months/year, 6 depletion passes per month
    a. Juveniles, electrofishing, HFE trigger, euthanasia, domestic or endangered animal consumption
    b. Juveniles, gill netting, HFE trigger, euthanasia, domestic or endangered animal consumption
    c. Juveniles, fish traps, HFE trigger, euthanasia, domestic or endangered animal consumption
    d. Adults, electrofishing, euthanasia, freeze, smoke, or fresh, human consumption
    e. Adults, electrofishing, euthanasia, freeze, domestic or endangered animal consumption
    f. Adults, gill netting, euthanasia, freeze or smoke or fresh, human consumption
    g. Adults, gill netting, euthanasia, freeze, domestic or endangered animal consumption
    h. Adults, electrofishing, live removal, stock tribal fish ponds
    i. Adults, gill netting, live removal, stock tribal fish ponds
    j. *And other possible options and combinations*
6. BNT removal from Bright Angel Creek (fish weir)
7. BNT removal expanded to multiple tributaries
8. BNT removal as standard operating procedure coinciding with monitoring activities

9. Stranding flows to reduce reproduction and recruitment (de-water redds). Similar to trout suppression flows of 2003–2005, but modified to be more effective (lower daily flow at 2,500 ft³/s). Period: Feb 1–Apr 30. Flow: Up to 20,000 ft³/s (17,500 ft³/s if maintenance limitations constrain operations) maximum daily flow for 13 days (min. daily flow doesn't matter). On day 14, drop flow to 2,500 to 5,000 ft³/s between 8 am–1 pm, then resume normal ROD operations. Repeat.
10. Increase daily downramp to strand or displace age-0 trout. Period: May 1–Aug 1. Flow: ROD operations but unrestricted downramp rates.
11. Stranding flows (high flow followed by low flow) to strand or displace age-0 trout. Period: May 1–Aug 1. Flow: High (20,000 ft³/s) for 2–4 days, followed by rapid decline to 2,500–5,000 ft³/s held for ½ to one day. Repeat (2 cycles/month = 6 cycles total).
12. Mechanical or chemical disruption of redds
13. Fine-sediment augmentation @ Paria River confluence
14. Lees Ferry fine sediment slurry (mitigates for HFE enhanced production response, RBT trigger – abundance or RBT juvenile survival)
15. Construction of some barrier to downstream movement of trout
16. Alter fishery to a stocked, non-productive fishery (triploid males)
17. Expand harvest of trout (reward program, tribal guides, other methods)
18. Headstarting (remove young HBC from the wild, grow in hatchery until large enough to avoid predation, then reintroduce in the wild)

5.3. Hybrid Portfolios

Single strategies can be combined to form hybrid portfolios, which represent alternatives for long-term management of the resources (table 3). The portfolios were built up from combinations of single strategies to emphasize certain objectives or actions. For example, a portfolio emphasizing cultural sensitivity during removal actions (hybrid portfolio C) was created by finding beneficial uses (live or lethal) for removed fish, using humane methods of capture and handling, and establishing triggers so the removal is minimized and restricted to when and where it is thought to be necessary for humpback chub recovery.

Table 3. Hybrid portfolios, composed of multiple single strategies (table 2), for removal or suppression of non-native fish, or enhancement of humpback chub populations.

[The key uncertainties and their relationships to the hybrid portfolios are more fully described in figure 4; RBT, rainbow trout; BNT, brown trout; LCR, Little Colorado River; HBC, humpback chub; PBR, Paria-to-Badger reach]

A. No action (single strategies: 1, 6)   Assumptions: RBT do not limit chub recovery, but BNT do.
B. Status quo (single strategies: 2, 6): 4.2 LCR trips per year   Assumptions: RBT and BNT limit chub recovery, RBT near LCR are self-sustaining or no other methods work to reduce RBT density at LCR, other objectives collectively outweigh tribal cultural concerns.
C_1. Culturally sensitive removal at LCR (single strategies: 3a, 6): 4.2 LCR trips per year   Assumptions: RBT and BNT limit chub recovery, RBT near LCR are self-sustaining or no other methods work to reduce RBT density at LCR, tribal concerns can be met through beneficial use.
C_2. Culturally sensitive removal at LCR (single strategies: 3b, 6): 4.2 LCR trips per year   Assumptions: see C_1.
C_3. Culturally sensitive removal at LCR (single strategies: 3a,b,e; 6): 4.2 LCR trips per year, 20 percent of trout removed alive (by helicopter), 20 percent smoked for human consumption, 60 percent frozen for animal consumption.   Assumptions: see C_1.
C_4. Culturally sensitive removal at LCR (single strategies: 3e, 6): 4.2 LCR trips per year, all trout removed alive by equipping boats with livewells and floating downstream, for stocking in tribal ponds.   Assumptions: see C_1.
C_5. Culturally sensitive removal at LCR (single strategies: 3e, 6): 4.2 LCR trips per year, all trout removed alive by helicopter, for use in tribal fish ponds.   Assumptions: see C_1.
D_1. Removal curtain (single strategies: 3b, 5e, 6): #5 is the long-term strategy to reduce emigration, but #3 is needed in short-term to reduce extant RBT population. Expect 1.6 LCR trips per year on average. All trout frozen and used for animal consumption.   Assumptions: RBT and BNT limit HBC recovery, Lees Ferry is the source of RBT, removal @ PBR effectively stops emigration.
D_2. Removal curtain (single strategies: 3b, 5h, 6): #5 is the long-term strategy to reduce emigration, but #3 is needed in short-term to reduce extant RBT population. Expect 1.6 LCR trips per year on average. Trout removed at LCR are frozen and used for animal consumption; at PBR, trout removed alive and used to stock tribal fish ponds.   Assumptions: see D_1.
D_3. Removal curtain (single strategies: 3e, 5h, 6): #5 is the long-term strategy to reduce emigration, but #3 is needed in short-term to reduce extant RBT population. Expect 1.6 LCR trips per year on average. All trout removed alive (use of helicopters at LCR) and used to stock tribal fish ponds.   Assumptions: see D_1.
E. Sediment curtain (single strategies: 3b, 5e, 6, 13): #13 is long-term strategy to emigration; #5 is the short-term strategy to emigration while infrastructure is being built; #3 is needed in short-term to reduce extant RBT population   Assumptions: RBT and BNT limit HBC recovery, Lees Ferry is the source of RBT, removal @ PBR or sediment curtain will work to reduce emigration; in the long-term, sediment curtain is cheaper than ongoing removal.

F. Stranding flow (single strategies: 6, 11)
    Assumptions: RBT and BNT limit chub recovery, Lees Ferry is the source of RBT and extant RBT population at LCR will disappear after migration is curtailed, stranding flows alone are sufficient to eliminate emigration
 	
    F'. Stranding flow with stocking of triploid males (single strategies: 6, 11, 16)
        Assumptions: RBT and BNT limit HBC recovery, Lees Ferry is the source of RBT and extant RBT population at LCR will disappear after migration is curtailed, stranding flows and stocking of triploid males are needed to eliminate emigration. This strategy could also arise if stranding flows alone are sufficient to reduce BRT production and emigration, but have a negative impact on fishery, which can be compensated

	for by stocking triploid males.
G.	Stranding flow with augmentation (single strategies: 5e, 6, 11): #11 is the long-term strategy to reduce production and emigration from Lees Ferry; #5 is used in the short-term to reduce emigration a bit quicker Assumptions: RBT limit HBC recovery; Lees Ferry is the source of RBT, stranding flows in combination with PBR will work to eliminate emigration, extant RBT population at LCR will disappear after migration is curtailed. G'. Stranding flow with augmentation and stocking of triploid males (single strategies: 5e, 6, 11, 16): #11 is the long-term strategy to reduce production and emigration from Lees Ferry; #5 is used in the short-term to reduce emigration a bit quicker Assumptions: RBT limit HBC recovery; Lees Ferry is the source of RBT, stranding flows in combination with PBR will work to eliminate emigration, extant RBT population at LCR will disappear after migration is curtailed, stranding flows have negative impact on fishery, which can be compensated for by stocking triploid males.
H.	Stranding flow with assurances (single strategies: 3b, 6, 11): #11 is the long-term strategy to reduce production and emigration from Lees Ferry; #3 is used in the short-term to reduce extant RBT population Assumptions: RBT limit HBC recovery, Lees Ferry is an important source of RBT, stranding is effective at eliminating emigration from Lees Ferry, but removal at LCR is needed to deal with extant RBT population and/or downstream self-sustaining RBT. H'. Stranding flow with assurances and stocking of triploid males (single strategies: 3b, 6, 11): #11 is the long-term strategy to reduce production and emigration from Lees Ferry; #3 is used in the short-term to reduce extant RBT population Assumptions: RBT limit HBC recovery, Lees Ferry is an important source of RBT, stranding is effective at eliminating emigration from Lees Ferry, but removal at LCR is needed to deal with extant RBT population and/or downstream self-sustaining RBT, stranding flows have negative impact on fishery, which can be compensated for by stocking triploid males.
I.	Dewater redds with assurances (single strategies: 5e, 6, 9) Assumptions: RBT limit HBC recovery, Lees Ferry is the source of RBT, dewatering works to some extent, but PBR removal is needed to remove the compensatory effect.
J_1.	Kitchen Sink I (single strategies: 3b, 5e, 6, 7, 8, 9, 10, 11): intended to reduce or eliminate the need for mechanical removal, by reducing trout recruitment and emigration through flow manipulation. Expect 1.3 LCR trips per year. All trout removed (LCR, PBR) frozen and used for animal consumption. Assumptions: RBT limit HBC recovery, Lees Ferry a primary source of RBT in LCR, little spawning by RBT south of Lees Ferry, BNT threaten chub recovery, HFE promote trout production, mechanical removal at LCR alone ineffective at maintain low trout abundance, flow manipulations can reduce recruitment and emigration of trout. J_1'. Kitchen Sink I with stocking of triploid males (single strategies: 3b, 5e, 6, 7, 8, 9, 10, 11, 16). Assumptions: see J_1. In addition, flow manipulations have a negative impact on trout fishery, which can be compensated by stocking triploid males.
J_2.	Kitchen Sink II (single strategies: 3e, 5h, 6, 7, 8, 9, 10, 11): intended to reduce or eliminate the need for mechanical removal, by reducing trout recruitment and emigration through flow manipulation. Expect 1.3 LCR trips per year. All trout removed alive and used to stock tribal fish ponds. Assumptions: see J_1. J_2'. Kitchen Sink II with stocking of triploid males (single strategies: 3e, 5h, 6, 7, 8, 9, 10, 11, 16). Assumptions: see J_1'.
K.	Zuni-Hopi-NPS strategy (single strategies: 5h, 6, 9, 17): Redd dewatering flows and expanded trout harvest at Lees Ferry to reduce trout emigration, with live removal at PBR to further reduce downstream emigration. No activity at LCR. Assumptions: (1) RBT not significantly limiting recruitment on HBC; HBC have survived in the system along with RBT for many decades. (temperature more a limiting factor than predation by RBT). High degree of uncertainty about relationship between RBT predation and recruitment; until resolved, not worth the other (spiritual) costs. (2) HBC range has decreased throughout the system (3) Life is sacred; unnecessary taking of life should not occur (4) RBT is a non-native in the system (Hopi perspective, not

	Zuni) (5) Human activity should be limited in the Grand Canyon (6) This is human caused situation – people caused the problem, now taking the easy way out but fish pay the penalty; human activities now having a negative cumulative effect on the whole system,
L.	Strategy K plus headstarting and barrier (single strategies: 5h, 6, 9, 15, 17, 18) Assumptions: (1) RBT not significantly limiting recruitment on HBC; HBC have survived in the system along with RBT for many decades. Temperature is a more limiting factor than predation by RBT. High degree of uncertainty about relationship between RBT predation and recruitment; until resolved, not worth the other (spiritual) costs.(2) HBC range has decreased throughout the system (3) Life is sacred; unnecessary taking of life should not occur (4) RBT is a non-native in the system (Hopi perspective, not Zuni) (5) Human activity should be limited in the Grand Canyon (6) This is human caused situation – people caused the problem, now taking the easy way out but fish pay the penalty; human activities now having a negative cumulative effect on the whole system, (7) additional actions (headstarting barrier) required.
M.	Selective-sacrifice and strand portfolio: (single strategies: 5j, 9 with trigger, (6): Portfolio is similar to stranding flow with assurances (H), but de-watering redds employed rather than flows to strand juveniles. Conduct stranding flows seasonally, approximately April–May. Assumptions: RBT limit HBC recovery, Lees Ferry is an important source of RBT, Lees Ferry is the source of RBT, stranding flows in combination with PBR will work to eliminate emigration, extant RBT population at LCR will disappear after migration is curtailed.
N.	BNT expanded removal (single strategies: 1, 3b, 6, 7, 8) Assumptions: BNT is large source of mortality on HBC, removal of BNT effective at maintaining high juv HBC survival, removal during monitoring trips will be effective at reducing BNT abundance, encounter rate consistent with on-site consumption.
O.	Expanded sediment curtain (single strategies: 3b, 5e, 6, 13, 14): sediment augmentation also introduced at Lees Ferry (#14), #13 is long-term solution to emigration; #5 is the short-term solution to emigration while infrastructure is being built; #3 is used to reduce extant RBT population Assumptions: RBT limit HBC recovery, Lees Ferry is the source of RBT, removal @ PBR stops emigration; sediment curtain will work to reduce emigration; in the long-term, sediment curtain is cheaper than ongoing removal.

Underlying each hybrid portfolio is a set of assumptions about how biological systems will respond to proposed actions. The consequences of the actions in terms of the objectives could differ depending on whether the assumptions hold or not. A diagram of critical assumptions relevant to this problem is shown in figure 4.

Workshop participants created 27 different hybrid portfolios representing a range of approaches, and an array of underlying assumptions (table 3). The portfolios can be grouped according to the basic underlying assumptions they rest on (fig. 4). Detailed narratives for the hybrid portfolios are found in appendix 2.

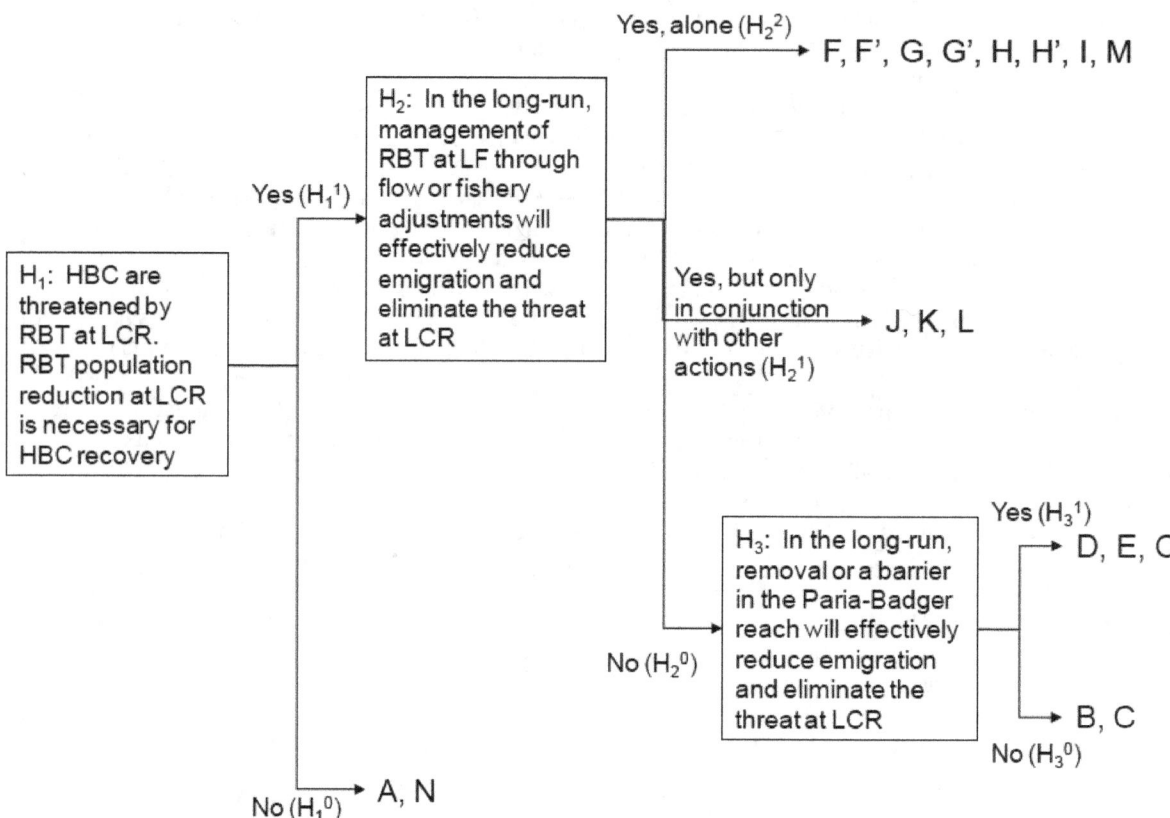

Figure 4. Flowchart showing key uncertainties in predicting the response of rainbow trout and humpback chub populations to management actions. The ends of the flowchart point to the hybrid portfolios (table 3) that are predicated on the series of hypotheses that lead to them. This flowchart is not, however, meant to be a decision tree, as the particular portfolios need not be favored even if the hypotheses on which they were created are true, owing to competing objectives.

5.4. Adaptive Strategies

If it were known which set of assumptions was valid, it would be easy to identify which hybrid portfolios were reliable candidates to carry forward in a decision analysis. In reality, there is uncertainty surrounding the underlying biological assumptions. Many of the stakeholders believe that the preferred approach will need to be adaptive, that is, it will need to entertain several hybrid portfolios as candidates, in a strategy that seeks to reduce uncertainty about the underlying mechanisms, and so identify the appropriate way forward to long-term management. An *adaptive strategy* may include experimental elements initially, but an important feature of an adaptive strategy is an understanding of which hybrid portfolio would eventually be adopted on a long-term basis once the relevant uncertainty has been acceptably resolved.

For example, one potential adaptive strategy was advanced by a group of scientists from GCMRC and elsewhere that met at any ecosystem modeling workshop in October 2010. This adaptive strategy can be characterized as including hybrid strategies {A, C, D}. This would be designed to test the assumptions about whether rainbow trout were limiting the LCR humpback chub population, and the effectiveness of removal in the PBR to stop emigration from Lees Ferry. If, after the next 1 to 2 years, rainbow trout in the LCR reach were found not to limit humpback chub, then hybrid Portfolio A would possibly be the best overall long-term management solution with respect to non-native fish control in the Canyon. If rainbow trout were found to limit humpback chub and removal in the PBR effectively stopped emigration, then hybrid Portfolio D would possibly be the best overall long-term solution. If rainbow trout were found to limit humpback chub and removal in the PBR was not effective, then hybrid Portfolio C would possibly be the best overall long-term management solution for non-native fish control.

Our view is that adaptive strategies should arise out of analysis of the hybrid portfolios and consideration of how key uncertainties affect the choice of a management option. Thus, development of adaptive strategies is discussed in section 7.4 after evaluation of the individual hybrid portfolios and a consideration of the expected value of information.

6. Consequences of the Hybrid Strategies

In a multi-criteria decision analysis, the evaluation stage consists of an examination of each of the alternatives against each of the objectives (as expressed by the measurable attributes). These *consequences* link the actions to the objectives and provide the basis for a trade-off analysis.

6.1. Methods

Four teams of experts were assembled to evaluate the consequences of the hybrid portfolios, a Cultural Objectives team, an Ecological Objectives team, a Recreational Objectives team, and a Public Service Objectives team. These teams reviewed the objectives, developed appropriate scales on which to measure achievement of those objectives (measurable attributes), and scored each hybrid portfolio against each of the measurable attributes. In some cases, the "scoring" was done through development of a quantitative model for predicting the outcomes associated with each alternative; in other cases, expert elicitation was employed to develop the scoring.

6.2. Evaluation of Cultural Objectives

The consequences for the cultural objectives (measurable attributes 1A–1D) are shown in table 4. Representatives from three Tribes (Hopi Tribe, Pueblo of Zuni, and Navajo Nation) attended the second workshop and participated in the assessment of consequences to cultural objectives. Given that each Tribe is a sovereign entity with a distinct perspective, their scores were treated separately in the analysis. All five tribes had been invited to participate in the discussions between workshops, but only the three above, plus the Hualapai representative, were able to provide feedback in the development of objectives and measurable attributes.

Table 4. Consequence matrix for cultural objectives.

[Scores are shown for three different Tribal perspectives (Zuni/Hopi/Navajo). Hybrid portfolios shaded in light green were included in the final analysis. Note that the measurable attributes changed between the initial and final analyses, and only the portfolios included in the final analysis were scored on the new scale. LCR, Little Colorado River; NPS, National Park Service; BNT, brown trout]

	Hybrid portfolio	1A: Avoid taking life	1B: Respect life	1C: Culturally appropriate	1D: Protect sanctity
		0–1	0–10	0–1	0–1
		Maximize	Maximize	Maximize	Maximize
A	No action	0 / 1 / 0	7 / 10 / 1	1 / 1 / 0	1 / 1 / 0
B	Status quo	ns[7]	0 / 9 / 1	ns	ns
C_1	LCR removal (3a)	ns	7 / 9 / 5	ns	ns
C_2	LCR removal (3b)	0 / 0 / 0	5 / 9 / 5	0 / 0.4 / 0	0 / 0.3 / 0
C_3	LCR removal (3abe)	0 / 0 / 0	5 / 9 / 5	0 / 0.4 / 0	0 / 0.2 / 0
C_4	LCR removal (3e, boat)	0 / 1 / 0	9 / 10 / 10	1 / 0.5 / 0	0 / 0.4 / 1
C_5	LCR removal (3e, helicopter)	0 / 1 / 0	9 / 10 / 10	1 / 0.5 / 0	0 / 0.1 / 1
D_1	Removal curtain (3b, 5e)	0 / 0 / 0	5 / 9 / 10	0 / 0.3 / 0	0 / 0.4 / 1
D_2	Removal curtain (3b, 5h)	0 / 0 / 0	5 / 9 / 5	0 / 0.3 / 0	0 / 0.4 / 1
D_3	Removal curtain (3e, 5h)	0 / 1 / 0	9 / 10 / 10	1 / 0.4 / 0	0 / 0.3 / 1
E	Sediment curtain	ns	5 / 10 / 10	ns	ns
F	Stranding flow	ns	5 / 3 / 10	ns	ns
F'	Stranding flow with triploid	ns	0 / 3 / 10	ns	ns
G	Stranding flow with augmentation	ns	2 / 3 / 10	ns	ns
G'	Stranding flow with augmentation and triploid	ns	2 / 3 / 10	ns	ns
H	Stranding flow with assurances	ns	0 / 9 / 10	ns	ns
H'	Stranding flow with assurances and triploid	ns	2 / 9 / 10	ns	ns
I	De-water redds	ns	3 / 3 / 10	ns	ns
J_1	Kitchen sink (3b, 5e)	0 / 0 / 0	0 / 0 / 5	0 / 0.2 / 1	0 / 0.2 / 1
J_1'	Kitchen sink (3b, 5e) with triploid	0 / 0 / 0	0 / 0 / 5	0 / 0.1 / 1	0 / 0.5 / 1

---

[7] Not scored in the final analysis.

Hybrid portfolio		1A: Avoid taking life	1B: Respect life	1C: Culturally appropriate	1D: Protect sanctity
		0–1	0–10	0–1	0–1
		Maximize	Maximize	Maximize	Maximize
J$_2$	Kitchen sink II (3e, 5h)	0 / 0 / 0	0 / 0 / 5	0 / 0.2 / 1	0 / 0.4 / 1
J$_2$'	Kitchen sink II (3e, 5h) with triploid	0 / 0 / 0	0 / 0 / 5	0 / 0.2 / 1	0 / 0.4 / 1
K	Zuni-Hopi-NPS	0 / 0 / 0	7 / 10 / 10	1 / 0.3 / 1	0 / 0.9 / 1
L	K + head-starting and barrier	ns	7 / 10 / 10	ns	ns
M	Selective-Sacrifice & Strand	ns	4 / 3 / 10	ns	ns
N	Expanded BNT	ns	7 / 9 / 10	ns	ns
O	Expanded sediment curtain	ns	3 / 3 / 10	ns	ns

The development of attributes for each of the cultural objectives proved somewhat difficult as there was reluctance to ascribe value or scalar levels to spirituality. This is entirely understandable. Perhaps a more efficient process would have been to develop other objectives that were less "fundamental" from a spiritual perspective and more akin to means objectives. For example, preserving the sanctity of the Canyon may have been easier to convey by describing this as "minimizing the footprint" of the proposed actions, which then could have led to the development of a scale measuring disturbance. The location of the action within the Canyon was considered, but this measure was less effective at supporting the fundamental objective because the entire Canyon is considered sacred. See section 8.2 for further comments on the process of scoring cultural objectives.

Between the initial analysis (conducted at the second workshop) and the final analysis, the set of alternatives being considered changed, and the interpretation of these four measurable attributes changed as well. The initial set of alternatives was never evaluated with the final interpretation of the attributes, so some scores are not shown in table 3. The interpretations that follow are for the final analysis only.

For attribute 1A, the Zuni and Navajo representatives simply evaluated whether life was being taken at all; since all of the alternatives involve some taking of life (note the no action alternative, A, includes brown and rainbow trout removal at Bright Angel Creek), all of them scored 0. The Hopi representative viewed the scale differently, and gave a score of 1 to those alternatives that took a minimum of life.

For attribute 1B, the tribal representatives interpreted the degree to which the beneficial use of any trout removed reflected a respect for life. Live removal options tended to score higher on this attribute, but there was a significant difference in how the three tribes scored this attribute.

For attribute 1C, the Zuni and Navajo representatives used a binary scale, evaluating whether the alternative was culturally appropriate or not. The Hopi representative used a continuous utility scale between 0 and 1 and applied fractional values for alternatives that would have intermediate value.

For attribute 1D, the Zuni and Navajo representatives used a binary scale, evaluating whether the alternative preserved the sanctity of the Canyon or not. The Hopi representative used a continuous utility scale between 0 and 1 and applied fractional values for alternatives that would have intermediate value.

6.3. Evaluation of Ecological Objectives

The consequences for the ecological objectives (measurable attributes 2A–2D) are shown in table 5. Three of these measurable attributes (2A, 2D1, and 2D2) were developed using predictive population models; the other four (2B1, 2B2, 2C1, and 2C2) were developed using a constructed scale.

Table 5. Consequence matrix for ecological objectives.

[HBC, humpback chub; NNF, non-native fish; yr, year; RBT, rainbow trout; LCR, Little Colorado River; NPS, National Park Service; BNT, brown trout]

Hybrid portfolio		2A: HBC recovery	2B1: Invasive species import	2B2: Invasive species export	2C1: Disease import	2C2: Disease export	2D1: NNF abund.	2D2: Native fish goals
		Pr(N greater than 6,000 for 30 yr)	Risk	Risk	Risk	Risk	RBT at LCR	Freq (HBC greater than 10,000)
		Maximize	Minimize	Minimize	Minimize	Minimize	Minimize	Maximize
A	No action	0.232	None	None	None	None	6,486	0.19
B	Status quo	0.346	Low	Low	Low	Low	4,673	0.25
C_1	LCR removal (3a)	0.341	Low	Low	Low	Low	4,673	0.26
C_2	LCR removal (3b)	0.341	Low	Low	Low	Low	4,673	0.26
C_3	LCR removal (3abe)	0.341	Low	High	Low	Med.	4,673	0.26
C_4	LCR removal (3e, boat)	0.341	Low	High	Low	Med.	4,673	0.26
C_5	LCR removal (3e, helicopter)	0.341	Low	High	Low	Med.	4,673	0.26
D_1	Removal curtain (3b, 5e)	0.532	Low	Low	Low	Low	827	0.39
D_2	Removal curtain (3b, 5h)	0.532	Low	High	Low	Med.	827	0.39
D_3	Removal curtain (3e, 5h)	0.532	Low	High	Low	Med.	827	0.39
E	Sediment curtain	0.557	Low	Low	Low	Low	333	0.43
F	Stranding flow	0.228	None	None	None	None	5,302	0.17

Hybrid portfolio		2A: HBC recovery	2B1: Invasive species import	2B2: Invasive species export	2C1: Disease import	2C2: Disease export	2D1: NNF abund.	2D2: Native fish goals
		Pr(N greater than 6,000 for 30 yr)	Risk	Risk	Risk	Risk	RBT at LCR	Freq (HBC greater than 10,000)
		Maximize	Minimize	Minimize	Minimize	Minimize	Minimize	Maximize
F'	Stranding flow with triploid	0.224	Med.	None	Low	Low	6,039	0.17
G	Stranding flow with augmentation	0.278	Low	Low	Low	Low	1,516	0.21
G'	Stranding flow with augmentation and triploid	0.279	Med.	Low	Med.	Low	1,662	0.21
H	Stranding flow with assurances	0.355	Low	Low	Low	Low	3,388	0.25
H'	Stranding flow with assurances and triploid	0.341	Med.	Low	Med.	Low	3,836	0.25
I	De-water redds	0.276	Low	Low	Low	Low	1,791	0.20
J_1	Kitchen sink (3b, 5e)	0.555	Low	Low	Low	Low	677	0.41
J_1'	Kitchen sink (3b, 5e) with triploid	0.536	Med.	Low	Med.	Low	697	0.41
J_2	Kitchen sink II (3e, 5h)	0.555	Low	High	Low	Med.	677	0.41
J_2'	Kitchen sink II (3e, 5h) with triploid	0.536	Med.	High	Med.	Med.	697	0.41
K	Zuni-Hopi-NPS	0.291	Low	High	Low	Med.	1,410	0.22
L	K + head-starting and barrier	--[8]	Med.	Low	Low	Low	--	--
M	Selective-Strand & Sacrifice	0.276	Low	Low	Low	Low	1,791	0.20
N	Expanded BNT	--	Low	Low	Low	Low	--	--

[8] Not enough detail was provided about Portfolios L and N to predict the trout and chub population responses.

Hybrid portfolio		2A: HBC recovery	2B1: Invasive species import	2B2: Invasive species export	2C1: Disease import	2C2: Disease export	2D1: NNF abund.	2D2: Native fish goals
		Pr(N greater than 6,000 for 30 yr)	Risk	Risk	Risk	Risk	RBT at LCR	Freq (HBC greater than 10,000)
		Maximize	Minimize	Minimize	Minimize	Minimize	Minimize	Maximize
O	Expanded sediment curtain	0.557	None	None	None	None	333	0.43

The predictive population models used to evaluate the consequences of policy alternatives on humpback chub and rainbow trout objectives (cf Section 4.3) involved a set of 3 coupled models (Lew Coggins, Service, and Josh Korman, Ecometric Research, Inc., oral commun., 2010). The elements of this coupled model included (1) emigration from the Lees Ferry tailwaters reach into Marble Canyon, (2) dynamics of rainbow trout during movement from Lees Ferry to LCR, and (3) the interaction between rainbow trout and humpback chub in the LCR confluence reach (fig. 5). This conceptual model provided the basic structure for development of a predictive model, which took as input the alternative hybrid portfolios, and produced as output the desired measurable attributes. Uncertainties were incorporated as stochastic parameters or as competing models with corresponding model weights (cf Section 6.6). The predictive model was implemented in an Excel spreadsheet and Monte Carlo-based estimates of expected responses were generated using a PopTools add-in. The results were projected over a 30-year time horizon, and means were calculated from 500 replicates of the stochastic model.

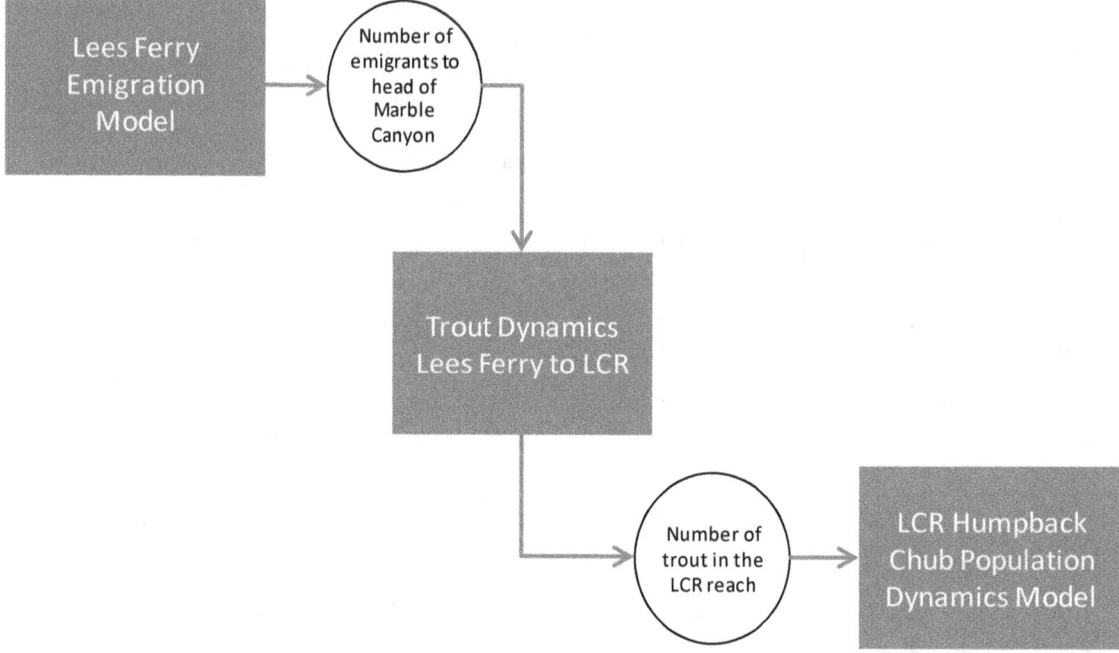

Figure 5. Conceptual model of fish community dynamics in the Colorado River below Glen Canyon Dam (Lew Coggins, Service, written commun., 2010). This provided the basis for a predictive model (Lew Coggins, Service, and Josh Korman, Ecometric Research, Inc., written commun., 2010) to support the decision analysis.

Rates of rainbow trout emigration from Lees Ferry into Marble Canyon were based on analysis of Lees Ferry recruitment in year t and monthly emigration in year $t + 1$. Base recruitment rates were modeled as a function of flow policy, and affect emigration rates. The Modified Low Fluctuating Flow (MLFF) record-of-decision operating strategy (U.S. Department of the Interior, 1996) provided the baseline recruitment and emigration rates. Alternative flow strategies (that is, de-watering redds and fry displacement or stranding flows) reduce recruitment and suppress emigration; however, high-flow experiments (HFEs) have been shown to increase recruitment and enhance emigration (table 6) as recently reported by Korman and others (2010). In the model, release of triploid males at Lees Ferry (in the stocking alternatives) increased baseline recruitment from 50 to 70 and 200 to 220 ($\times 1,000$) under the "Without HFE" and "With HFE" scenarios, respectively.

Table 6. Predictions of Lees Ferry rainbow trout recruitment and emigration to Marble Canyon as affected by flow policies, and incorporated into the model to predict consequences of alternatives on ecological objectives.

[Predictions are based on analyses that fit a monthly stock assessment model to monitoring data from the Lees Ferry tailwaters reach and Marble Canyon (Josh Korman, Ecometric Research, Inc., oral commun., 2010); ROD, 1996 Record of Decision]

Flow policy	Recruitment reduction	Monthly emigration (x1,000)	
		Without high flow experiment	With high flow experiment
Modified Low Fluctuating Flow (1996 ROD)	0.00	1.95	7.20
Dewatering redds	0.10	1.78	6.50
Rapid downramping	0.30	1.43	5.10
Stranding flows	0.40	1.25	4.40
All suppression flows combined	0.62	0.86	2.85

Movement of rainbow trout through reaches within Marble Canyon was modeled on a monthly time step. Each reach was defined to have a 'carrying capacity' so that excess abundance 'spilled over' into the adjacent downstream reach. In addition, stochastic movement was modeled to be independent of reach-specific abundance. Baseline monthly survival rate was 0.97. Reach-specific abundance was affected by alternatives that included removal, whether from the Paria River to Badger Creek reach (PBR, RM 0 to 8), or from the reach near the LCR (Kwagunt Canyon to Lava Canyon reach, RM 56 to 66). The magnitude of removal was a function of capture probability, number of passes per trip, and number of months when removal occurred. Capture probability was 0.15 based on prior removal experiments. Optionally, removal was triggered by a critical abundance of rainbow trout within the respective reach. Fine-sediment augmentation implemented to increase turbidity in Marble Canyon lowered the monthly survival rate to 0.85.

An age-structured model was used to predict the dynamics of humpback chub in the LCR and adjacent mainstem habitats. Movement of juveniles from the LCR to the mainstem was on a half-year time step over the 4 years prior to maturity. The interaction between humpback chub and rainbow trout was modeled to occur in the mainstem habitats. Survival of juvenile humpback chub was modeled as a logistic function of rainbow-trout abundance within the Kwagunt Canyon to Lava Canyon reach. The logistic function was tuned to generate on average 10,000 adult humpback chub in the absence of an rainbow-trout effect (RBT hypothesis false) and 2,500 adult humpback chub for a maximum rainbow-trout effect (RBT hypothesis true). The logistic function could be turned off to model humpback chub dynamics as independent of rainbow-trout abundance. The predicted response of humpback chub to each alternative hybrid portfolio is shown in table 7, as a function of all combinations of the three underlying hypotheses (see section 6.6 for discussion of the three hypotheses).

Table 7. Predicted humpback chub response as a function of the combinations of three hypotheses.

[The response variable shown is the probability of the humpback chub population at the Lower Colorado River reach remaining above 6,000 adults for a 30-year period. The hypotheses concern (1) the effect of high-flow experimental releases (HFE) on trout recruitment and emigration, (2) the effect of rainbow trout on humpback chub (RBT), and (3) the effectiveness of specific flow regime to reduce trout recruitment and emigration (Flow). The weight on the eight combinations is found from the expert-elicited weight on the individual hypotheses. Pink shading shows the worst performing alternative under a particular combination of hypotheses, light green shows the best.]

HFE	No	No	No	No	Yes	Yes	Yes	Yes	
RBT	No	No	Yes	Yes	No	No	Yes	Yes	
Flow	No	Yes	No	Yes	No	Yes	No	Yes	
Weight	0.050	0.124	0.094	0.233	0.050	0.124	0.094	0.233	Average
Alternative									
A	0.660	0.660	0.010	0.010	0.660	0.660	0.000	0.000	0.232
C$_2$	0.660	0.660	0.344	0.344	0.660	0.660	0.000	0.000	0.341
C$_3$	0.660	0.660	0.344	0.344	0.660	0.660	0.000	0.000	0.341
C$_4$	0.660	0.660	0.344	0.344	0.660	0.660	0.000	0.000	0.341
C$_5$	0.660	0.660	0.344	0.344	0.660	0.660	0.000	0.000	0.341
D$_1$	0.660	0.660	0.509	0.509	0.660	0.660	0.418	0.418	0.532
D$_2$	0.660	0.660	0.509	0.509	0.660	0.660	0.418	0.418	0.532
D$_3$	0.660	0.660	0.509	0.509	0.660	0.660	0.418	0.418	0.532
J$_1$	0.660	0.660	0.509	0.525	0.660	0.660	0.418	0.502	0.555
J$_1$'	0.660	0.660	0.479	0.499	0.660	0.660	0.391	0.468	0.536
J$_2$	0.660	0.660	0.509	0.525	0.660	0.660	0.418	0.502	0.555
J$_2$'	0.660	0.660	0.479	0.499	0.660	0.660	0.391	0.468	0.536
K	0.660	0.660	0.100	0.110	0.660	0.660	0.048	0.098	0.291

The consequences of the alternatives to the risks and impacts of disease and invasive species (attributes 2B1, 2B2, 2C1, and 2C2) were derived from expert elicitation (Larry Riley and Bill Stewart, Arizona Game and Fish Department, written commun., 2010). For attribute 2B1 (the risk of invasive species import), the factors that increase the risk of import of an invasive species include the transportation of live fish to Glen or Grand Canyon from an outside location. Much of the risk can be controlled through use of preventative measures, but there is some inherent risk. For attribute 2B2 (the risk of invasive species export), the factors that increase the risk of export of resident unwanted species (such as New Zealand mudsnail and didymo) include the removal of live fish from Glen or Grand Canyon and transportation to other locations. The probability of mudsnail transport is high and their prevalence is high. Some degree of control can be exerted through control of destination. Any portfolio that includes the removal of live trout would score high based on these assumptions.

For attribute 2C1 (the risk of disease import), the factors that increase the risk of import of a disease agent include the transportation of live fish to Glen or Grand Canyon from an outside location. Much of the risk can be controlled through use of preventative measures, but there is some inherent risk. For attribute 2C2 (the risk of disease export), the factors that increase the risk of export of wildlife disease agents/parasites (Whirling Disease, Asian tapeworm, trout nematode) include the transportation of live (and sometimes dead) fish from Glen or Grand Canyon to other locations. Although there is uncertainty about the prevalence of Whirling Disease, it is assumed to be uncommon. Other parasites are fairly common.

6.4. Evaluation of Recreational Objectives

The consequences for the recreational objectives (measurable attributes 3A–3D) are shown in table 8.

Table 8. Consequence matrix for recreational objectives.

[LF, Lees Ferry; GCNRA, Glen Canyon National Recreation Area; hr, hour; yr, year; LCR, Little Colorado River; NPS, National Park Service; BNT, brown trout]

Hybrid portfolio		3A1: LF catch rate	3A2: LF size distri-bution	3B: Wilderness disturbance	3C: Wilderness boating experience	3D: GCNRA boating experience
		Fish/hr	Percent greater than 20 in.	Penalized user-days/yr	Days/yr within specifications	Days/yr within specifications
		Maximize	Maximize	Minimize	Maximize	Maximize
A	No action	0.76	0.05	0	365	365
B	Status quo	0.76	0.05	4,991	365	365
C_1	LCR removal (3a)	0.76	0.05	5,003	365	365
C_2	LCR removal (3b)	0.76	0.05	5,003	365	365
C_3	LCR removal (3abe)	0.76	0.05	5,037	365	365
C_4	LCR removal (3e, boat)	0.76	0.05	5,003	365	365
C_5	LCR removal (3e, helicopter)	0.76	0.05	5,154	365	365
D_1	Removal curtain (3b, 5e)	0.76	0.05	6,824	365	365
D_2	Removal curtain (3b, 5h)	0.76	0.05	6,824	365	365
D_3	Removal curtain (3e, 5h)	0.76	0.05	6,867	365	365
E	Sediment curtain	0.76	0.05	3,442	365	365
F	Stranding flow	0.46	2.5	0	359	359
F'	Stranding flow with triploid	0.76	1.0	0	359	359
G	Stranding flow with augmentation	0.46	2.5	2,700	359	359
G'	Stranding flow with augmentation and triploid	0.76	1.0	2,700	364	359

Hybrid portfolio		3A1: LF catch rate	3A2: LF size distribution	3B: Wilderness disturbance	3C: Wilderness boating experience	3D: GCNRA boating experience
		Fish/hr	Percent greater than 20 in.	Penalized user-days/yr	Days/yr within specifications	Days/yr within specifications
		Maximize	Maximize	Minimize	Maximize	Maximize
H	Stranding flow with assurances	0.46	2.5	4,596	364	359
H'	Stranding flow with assurances and triploid	0.76	1.0	5,051	364	359
I	De-water redds	0.68	0.5	2,700	364	362
J_1	Kitchen sink (3b, 5e)	0.29	2.5	6,753	359	354
J_1'	Kitchen sink (3b, 5e) with triploid	0.76	1.0	6,777	359	354
J_2	Kitchen sink II (3e, 5h)	0.29	2.5	6,793	359	354
J_2'	Kitchen sink II (3e, 5h) with triploid	0.76	1.0	6,818	359	354
K	Zuni-Hopi-NPS	0.46	1.0	5,400	364	354
L	K + head-starting and barrier	0.46	1.0	5,400	364	354
M	Selective-Strand & Sacrifice	0.46	2.5	5,400	364	354
N	Expanded BNT	0.76	0.05	--	365	365
O	Expanded sediment curtain	0.11	1.0	3,442	365	365

The results for attributes 3A1 (catch rate) and 3A2 (size distribution) were based on mean rates over the past 10 years (catch rate 0.76 fish/hr from creel surveys, 0.05 percent trout greater than 20" from electrofishing surveys, Bill Stewart, Arizona Game and Fish Department, written commun., 2010). It was assumed that these rates would remain the same for all portfolios that focused only on activities downstream of Lees Ferry (Portfolios A, B, C, D, E, N). For the various flow regimes in which stocking was not included (Portfolios F, G, H, M), it was assumed the trout recruitment at Lees Ferry would decline by 40 percent (Josh Korman, Ecometric Research, Inc., oral commun., 2010), and catch rates would decline similarly (to 0.46/hr), but the frequency of large fish would increase (to 2.5 percent) because of reduced intraspecific competition. For the portfolios that included stocking (F', G', H', J_1', J_2'), it was assumed the fish stocking would be at a level to return the catch rates to baseline (0.76/hr), even with reduced recruitment, but that the stocking would increase intraspecific competition so the frequency of large fish would drop to 1 percent. For the remaining portfolios (I, J_1, J_2, K, L, and O), the catch rate was assumed to decline to the same degree that the flow or sediment regimes reduced the age-0 recruitment, and the frequency of large fish would generally increase with decreases in catch rate, as a result of reduced intraspecific competition.

The consequences for attribute 3B (wilderness disturbance) were developed using the penalized user-days scale described in section 4.3. The number of LCR removal trips per year (where applicable) was predicted by the rainbow trout model used for attribute 2A (because trout removal is only triggered when the rainbow trout population exceeds 1,200 in the LCR removal reach). LCR removal trips were assumed to be 19 days long, with a staff of 14 taking half of the trips during the non-motor season and half during the motor season, and with all removal work done at night. For live removal from the LCR, it was assumed that a helicopter could move two drums per trip, each with 50 trout in it, and that approximately 1,800 trout would be removed per LCR trip. The number of PBR removal trips per year (where applicable) was assumed to be fixed at 10 per year, of 15 days in duration, and using a staff of eight. In the PBR, live removal can occur much more easily without helicopter support.

The consequences for attributes 3C (wilderness boating experience) and 3D (recreation area boating experience) were developed by estimating the number of days per year that conditions would remain within the parameters specified by the measurable attributes (see section 4.3). For attribute 3D, the following assumptions were made. First, many of the portfolios do not employ flow changes, so the expected number of days per year within the boating specifications is 365 (this assumes that current flow conditions allow for 365 boatable days per year). For the stranding flow portfolios (F, G, H), 6 days per year were anticipated to have flows greater than 3,000 ft^3/s for ½ day during daylight hours. For the de-watering redd portfolios (I, K, L, M), flows are restricted to less than 3,000 ft^3/s for ½ day on 3 days per year (once per month, February–April) during daylight hours. For the kitchen sink portfolios (J$_1$, J$_2$), three de-watering events and six stranding events per year are assumed, each of ½ day duration with flows less than 3,000 ft^3/s. In all cases, if the low flows are 5,000 ft^3/s rather than 3,000 ft^3/s, the boating conditions would not be affected, and the days per year within the specifications would remain at 365. With regard to the Lees Ferry sediment curtain (Portfolio O), it is difficult to know the effect on boating in the area. Certainly water clarity might change, which may modify some aspects of recreational experience. Turbid water conditions would not make navigational hazards, but they would make them harder to see for boaters.

6.5. Evaluation of Public Service Objectives

The consequences for the public service objectives (measurable attributes 4A–4F) are shown in table 9.

Table 9. Consequence matrix for economic and public service objectives.

[NNF, non-native fish; M$, million dollars; yr, year; LCR, Little Colorado River; NPS, National Park Service; BNT, brown trout]

Hybrid portfolio		4A: Economic value of fishery	4B: Economic value of wilder-ness	4C: Cost of NNF manage-ment[9]	4D: Impacts to Dam operation	4E: Power production	4F: Impacts to water delivery
		M$/yr	M$/yr	M$ over 5-yr	Yes/No	M$/yr (relative)	Yes/No
		Maximize	**Maximize**	**Minimize**	**Minimize**	**Maximize**	**Minimize**
A	No action	$7.67	nc[10]	$0.00	No	0	No
B	Status quo	$7.67	nc	$3.13	No	0	No
C_1	LCR removal (3a)	$7.67	nc	$3.17	No	0	No
C_2	LCR removal (3b)	$7.67	nc	$3.17	No	0	No
C_3	LCR removal (3abe)	$7.67	nc	$3.53	No	0	No
C_4	LCR removal (3e, boat)	$7.67	nc	$3.38	No	0	No
C_5	LCR removal (3e, helicopter)	$7.67	nc	$4.65	No	0	No
D_1	Removal curtain (3b, 5e)	$7.67	nc	$3.47	No	0	No
D_2	Removal curtain (3b, 5h)	$7.67	nc	$3.98	No	0	No
D_3	Removal curtain (3e, 5h)	$7.67	nc	$4.36	No	0	No
E	Sediment curtain	$7.67	nc	$436.78	No	0	No
F	Stranding flow	$4.60	nc	$0.00	No	−0.25	Yes
F'	Stranding flow with triploid	$7.67	nc	$0.18	No	−0.25	Yes
G	Stranding flow with augmentation	$4.60	nc	$1.29	No	−0.25	Yes
G'	Stranding flow with augmentation and triploid	$7.67	nc	$1.46	No	−0.25	Yes
H	Stranding flow with assurances	$7.67	nc	$2.92	No	−0.25	Yes
H'	Stranding flow with assurances	$7.67	nc	$3.38	No	−0.25	Yes

[9] This is the cost to Reclamation and the GCDAMP and does not include costs to other agencies or entities.

[10] Not calculated. The value to the local economy of wilderness experiences is not expected to be affected by the alternative portfolios, so this assessment was not completed in full.

Hybrid portfolio		4A: Economic value of fishery	4B: Economic value of wilder-ness	4C: Cost of NNF manage-ment[9]	4D: Impacts to Dam operation	4E: Power production	4F: Impacts to water delivery
		M$/yr	M$/yr	M$ over 5-yr	Yes/No	M$/yr (relative)	Yes/No
		Maximize	Maximize	Minimize	Minimize	Maximize	Minimize
	and triploid						
I	De-water redds	$6.90	nc	$1.29	No	1.0	Yes
J_1	Kitchen sink (3b, 5e)	$2.93	nc	$3.43	No	2.00	Yes
J_1'	Kitchen sink (3b, 5e) with triploid	$7.67	nc	$3.62	No	2.00	Yes
J_2	Kitchen sink II (3e, 5h)	$2.93	nc	$4.08	No	2.00	Yes
J_2'	Kitchen sink II (3e, 5h) with triploid	$7.67	nc	$4.32	No	2.00	Yes
K	Zuni-Hopi-NPS	$4.60	nc	$3.03	No	1.00	Yes
L	K + head-starting and barrier	$4.60	nc	nc[11]	No	1.00	Yes
M	Selective-Strand & Sacrifice	$4.60	nc	$2.99	No	1.0	Yes
N	Expanded BNT	$7.67	nc	nc	No	0	No
O	Expanded sediment curtain	$1.07	nc	$594.78	No	0	No

The results for measurable attribute 4A (economic value of the Lees Ferry fishery) were based on the mean angler days per year (1967–97, McKinney and Persons, 1999; and 2001, Silberman, 2003) and the average expenditures per angler-day ($210/day, Silberman, 2003) for a base rate of $7.67 million per year. It was then assumed that angler-days are proportional to the catch rate (McKinney and Persons, 1999), and the economic values were adjusted in proportion to the catch rates (attribute 3A1).

As noted above, the economic value of wilderness recreation (attribute 4B) was not expected to differ across alternative portfolios. The demand for the wilderness experience exceeds availability (with limited permits for boat trips issued each year), so any changes to the wilderness experience brought about by the alternatives considered here were assumed to have a negligible effect on the recreational use and its local economic benefits.

The results for measurable attribute 4C (cost of non-native fish management) were developed by building up the costs associated with the components of the hybrid portfolios. The following assumptions about costs formed the basis of this calculation. The number of LCR removal trips per year (where applicable) was predicted by the rainbow trout model used for attribute 2A (because trout removal is only triggered when the rainbow trout population exceeds 1,200 in the LCR removal reach). For live removal from the LCR, it was assumed that a helicopter could move two drums per trip, each

---

[11] Not enough detail was specified for Portfolios L and N to calculate the costs of implementation.

containing 50 trout, and that approximately 1,800 trout would be removed per LCR trip. The number of PBR removal trips per year (where applicable) was assumed to be fixed at 10 per year. Each LCR river trip was assumed to cost $150,000, each PBR trip $50,000. Helicopter use was assumed to cost $3,500 per trip in and out of the canyon (approximately 1 hour). The costs for various beneficial uses were as follows: use of a smoker, $1,500 per trip; use of a freezer, $5,000 per year plus $500 per trip; use of a livewell, $2,000 per trip; cost to transport and place live fish in tribal stocking ponds, $5 per fish. The cost of stocking triploid male trout in Lees Ferry was estimated at $35,000 per year. Previous studies have estimated the cost of construction and operation of fine-sediment slurry pipelines: a pipeline to Paria River has an estimated construction cost of $380 million and an annual operational cost of $11 million; a fine-sediment slurry pipeline to just below Glen Canyon Dam has an estimated construction cost of $140 million and an annual operational cost of $3.6 million (Randle and others, 2007).

The results for measurable attribute 4D (impacts on dam operation) were evaluated by Reclamation staff. The assessment was made that none of the proposed alternatives would have a negative effect on dam operation.

The results for measurable attribute 4E (effect on power production) were developed by staff from the WAPA, and represent the change in the economic value of power production at Glen Canyon Dam relative to current conditions. A number of the alternatives that allow for high ramping rates provide the opportunity for an increase in power generation, while those that impose fixed flows for long periods reduce the power generation potential.

The results for measurable attribute 4F (impacts to water delivery) were developed by staff from the Reclamation and reflect expert judgment about whether the alternatives will require Reclamation to reallocate monthly obligations for water delivery. All of the alternatives that involve changes to flows have the potential to alter water delivery to some extent.

The consequences for the strategic objectives (measurable attributes 5A–5D) are shown in table 10. These were developed by Reclamation staff and show a tentative judgment about the degree to which the alternative portfolios are likely to meet these obligations.

Table 10. Consequence matrix for strategic objectives.

[ESA, Endangered Species Act of 1973; HFE, high-flow experiment; LCR, Little Colorado River; NPS, National Park Service; BNT, brown trout]

Hybrid portfolio		5A: Maintain compliance with ESA	5B: Remain within Reclamation authority	5C: Support the HFE protocol	5D: Recognize Trust responsibilities
		0/1/2	Yes/No	Yes/No	0/1/2
		Max	Max	Max	Max
A	No action	0	Yes	No	ns[12]
B	Status quo	2	Yes	Yes	ns
C_1	LCR removal (3a)	2	Yes	Yes	ns
C_2	LCR removal (3b)	2	Yes	Yes	ns
C_3	LCR removal (3abe)	2	Yes	Yes	ns
C_4	LCR removal (3e, boat)	2	Yes	Yes	ns
C_5	LCR removal (3e, helicopter)	2	Yes	Yes	ns
D_1	Removal curtain (3b, 5e)	2	Yes	Yes	ns
D_2	Removal curtain (3b, 5h)	2	Yes	Yes	ns
D_3	Removal curtain (3e, 5h)	2	Yes	Yes	ns
E	Sediment curtain	2	No	Yes	ns
F	Stranding flow	0	Yes	No	ns
F'	Stranding flow with triploid	0	No	No	ns
G	Stranding flow with augmentation	1	Yes	No	ns
G'	Stranding flow with augmentation and triploid	1	No	No	ns
H	Stranding flow with assurances	2	Yes	Yes	ns
H'	Stranding flow with assurances and triploid	2	No	Yes	ns
I	De-water redds	1	Yes	No	ns

[12] Not scored. At the time of analysis, scores had not been developed for this attribute.

Hybrid portfolio		5A: Maintain compliance with ESA	5B: Remain within Reclamation authority	5C: Support the HFE protocol	5D: Recognize Trust responsibilities
		0/1/2	Yes/No	Yes/No	0/1/2
		Max	Max	Max	Max
J₁	Kitchen sink (3b, 5e)	1	No	No	ns
J₁'	Kitchen sink (3b, 5e) with triploid	1	No	No	ns
J₂	Kitchen sink II (3e, 5h)	1	No	No	ns
J₂'	Kitchen sink II (3e, 5h) with triploid	1	No	No	ns
K	Zuni-Hopi-NPS	1	No	No	ns
L	K + head-starting and barrier	1	No	No	ns
M	Selective-Strand & Sacrifice	1	Yes	No	ns
N	Expanded BNT	1	Yes	No	ns
O	Expanded sediment curtain	2	No	Yes	ns

6.6. Estimation of the Likelihood of the Assumptions

Several key uncertainties could affect optimal non-native fish control (fig. 4). Uncertainty around three hypotheses was deliberately defined, quantified, and incorporated into the decision analysis. The hypotheses are described below, as are the methods used to gauge the uncertainty about these hypotheses.

Hypothesis 1 (HFE hypothesis): high-flow experimental releases from Glen Canyon Dam will increase and sustain rainbow trout production in the Lees Ferry tailwaters reach at the levels seen in 2008 and 2009. When spring high-flow experiments were conducted in the past, there is evidence that trout productivity increased substantially, perhaps as a result of cleansing of the Glen Canyon river bed and other effects. In the March 2008 HFE, there is strong evidence that the effect was caused by the HFE, but the evidence is not as compelling for the March 1996 HFE (Korman and others, 2010). Whether these effects would be sustained over a long period of HFEs is not known. Uncertainty was characterized by specifying two competing models: in the null model (or if HFEs are not used), production in (and hence emigration from) Lees Ferry will continue at the base levels seen in the past decade (2000-10). In the alternative model, HFEs, released annually on average, will result in increased and sustained production and emigration of rainbow trout at levels consistent with the observations after recent spring high-flows (Korman, 2009).

Hypothesis 2 (RBT hypothesis): rainbow trout limit recovery of humpback chub through predation on juvenile chub, resource competition, and displacement. As noted earlier, there is empirical evidence that rainbow trout prey on juvenile chub (Yard and others, in press), and there is circumstantial evidence that trout removal efforts have benefited the humpback chub population at the LCR confluence (Coggins and others, in press). However, the strength of evidence for trout limitation of humpback chub is questioned by a number of the stakeholders in this process, as well as aquatic scientists conducting monitoring and research in collaboration with the GCMRC staff. Again, two competing models were used to characterize uncertainty. In the null model, juvenile humpback chub survival is not affected by the abundance of trout at the LCR; in the alternative model, juvenile humpback chub survival is a steep negative logistic function of trout abundance near the LCR confluence.

Hypothesis 3 (flow hypothesis): flow regimes (for example, de-watering redds, stranding juveniles) are effective in reducing rainbow trout production and emigration downstream from Lees Ferry into Marble and Grand Canyons. A number of alternative portfolios were proposed that were designed to reduce the trout pressure at LCR by reducing production at, and emigration from, the Lees Ferry trout population, but these methods are untested. Again, two competing models were used to characterize uncertainty. In the null model, flow regimes had no effect on Lees Ferry tailwaters reach rainbow trout production and emigration rates. In the alternative model, monthly survival and emigration rates were reduced by flow-suppression strategies.

To quantify the uncertainties around these three key uncertainties, a panel of experts was asked to assess the evidence and place weight on the two competing models for each hypothesis. This expert elicitation process used a modified Delphi method (Kuhnert and others, 2010), and involved the elicitation of four points of information (Speirs-Bridge and others, 2010): the lower limit on the range of the elicited uncertainty, the upper limit on the range of the elicited uncertainty, the most likely (or best) value for the elicited uncertainty, and the confidence that the range includes the true uncertainty. The panel consisted of scientists with specific expertise in rainbow trout and humpback chub dynamics in the Colorado River, from USGS (Michael D. Yard, Theodore S. Melis, John F. Hamill), Ecometric Research, Inc. (Joshua Korman), the Service (Lewis G. Coggins, Jr.,) Reclamation (Glen W. Knowles), AZGF (Andrew S. Makinster), and WAPA (Shane Capron).

The ranges of uncertainty specified by the experts were standardized to 80-percent confidence interval, by assuming that their ranges followed a normal distribution, and the best values and 80-percent confidence bounds were averaged across experts (table 11). The average support for the HFE hypothesis was 0.50 (0.194–0.715), mostly reflecting that there has only been one documented, but unreplicated, spring-timed HFE followed by significantly increased rainbow trout production (Korman and others, 2010, in press). The average support for the RBT hypothesis was 0.653 (0.463–0.780), mostly reflecting a relatively large data set on rainbow trout predation (Yard and others, in press) and recent, but as yet unpublished data indicating that food production is limited in the main channel and that rainbow trout and humpback chub are known to compete for the same few taxa in the LCR confluence reach (T. Kennedy, Grand Canyon Monitoring and Research Center, oral commun., 2010). The average support for the flow hypothesis was 0.713 (0.553–0.822), mostly reflecting 2 years of experimental results reported by Korman (2009) when winter fluctuating flows were increased in 2003–04 to test a variant of the flow hypothesis relative to rainbow trout spawning, survival and recruitment (Korman and others, in press).

Table 11. Expert elicitation of the weight of evidence in favor of three underlying hypotheses.

[The four-point elicitation method was used, and the ranges were adjusted to an 80-percent confidence interval, assuming a normal distribution. The capital letters refer to individual experts.]

Expert	Four-point elicitation				Adjusted 80-percent confidence interval	
	Low	High	Best	Confidence	Low	High
HFE Hypothesis						
A	0.4	0.6	0.5	50	0.310	0.690
B	0.25	0.6	0.5	80	0.250	0.600
C	0.3	0.8	0.65	60	0.117	0.878
D	0.2	0.6	0.35	70	0.165	0.659
H	0.2	0.7	0.5	70	0.129	0.747
Average			**0.5**		**0.194**	**0.715**
Rainbow Trout Hypothesis						
A	0.3	0.5	0.4	50	0.210	0.590
B	0.55	0.85	0.7	80	0.550	0.850
C	0.3	0.7	0.6	80	0.300	0.700
D	0.3	0.9	0.66	95	0.425	0.817
E	0.6	0.95	0.8	90	0.644	0.917
F	0.4	0.8	0.66	80	0.400	0.800
G	0.7	0.8	0.75	90	0.711	0.789
Average			**0.653**		**0.463**	**0.780**
Flow Hypothesis						
A	0.7	0.8	0.75	90	0.711	0.789
B	0.6	0.8	0.7	80	0.600	0.800
C	0.4	0.8	0.7	80	0.400	0.800
D	0.5	0.9	0.7	80	0.500	0.900
Average			**0.7125**		**0.553**	**0.822**

Elicitation included discussion to identify important factors likely to affect the expert's opinion regarding the source and level of uncertainty. Regarding the effect of rainbow trout on humpback chub, experts discussed the evidence for mechanisms (such as predation and competition) and concurrent trends in monitoring data. Regarding flow regimes, experts stressed importance of the level of low flows on rainbow trout production, and that their opinions were based on an assumed low flow of 2,500 ft^3/s, relative to the 5,000 ft^3/s low flows that were actually experimentally evaluated in winters of 2003–04. Also, the experts emphasized that the design of the flow regimes should take advantage of observed fish behavior and interaction with bank morphology, namely low angle compared to high angle shoreline habitats.

The elicitation on HFEs focused on the ecological effect of relatively more frequent HFEs in the context of a future long-term sandbar conservation flow experiment on rainbow trout production and subsequent emigration and ignored the uncertainty regarding whether or not an HFE policy would be implemented. Thus, the experts were asked to express their uncertainty regarding ecological effects given that HFEs would be implemented on a frequent basis, such as annually or near annually. The discussion assumed a sediment-based policy, which would call for a 1/3 spring and 2/3 fall implementation schedule, estimated on the basis of historical annual Paria River sand production data.

The experts acknowledged greater evidence for effects on rainbow trout from spring HFE compared to fall HFE. However, the consensus was that a fall HFE event could also increase trout production.

Note that uncertainty concerning whether rainbow trout removal at PBR would be effective in reducing emigration and trout abundance at LCR was not formally analyzed. The predictive models for rainbow trout and humpback chub abundance assumed that PBR removal activities would be effective in removing a large number of rainbow trout in the PBR, and therefore, emigration downstream would be reduced considerably.

7. Decision Analysis

Multi-criteria decision analysis methods were used to evaluate the consequences of the proposed hybrid portfolios. At the second workshop, 20 hybrid portfolios were included in the analysis, objective weights were elicited from the agency and Tribal representatives, and the results were discussed (these results are not included in this report). A number of portfolios (B, C1, F, F', G, G', H, H', I, M) were eliminated from further consideration because their performance was robustly poor. Several others (L, N) were eliminated because the details of them were not well developed and they could not be evaluated. Finally, two high-ranking portfolios (E, O) were eliminated from further consideration because of their exorbitant cost and because they were clearly outside the scope of this EA. An additional seven hybrid portfolios were created (mostly permutations of C, D, and J), and a total of 13 portfolios were carried forward for final analysis.

7.1. Swing Weighting

Weights on 20 objectives (1A through 4F, less 4B and 4D) were elicited from the agencies and Tribes who had been present at the second workshop through a process called swing weighting (von Winterfeldt and Edwards, 1986). Weights were assigned on the basis of the absolute importance of the objective in question as well as the range of values over which the attribute varied across alternatives. Because of the large number of objectives, the swing weighting was conducted in a hierarchical manner, with attributes clustered into eight major categories according to relatedness of the objectives and correlation in the attributes.

In addition to weights on the objectives, the representatives were asked to assign weights to the three cultural tables, and to the three hypotheses. It's important to note that these tasks are all quite distinct. In the objective weighting, the representatives were asked to express how their agency or Tribe values the objectives relative to one another. In the weighting of the cultural tables, the representatives were asked how well they felt the three tables represented the cultural values that were at stake in this question. In weighting the hypotheses, the representatives were evaluating the scientific evidence in favor of the system dynamics they captured.

The results of these elicitations are shown in table 12. Most of the representatives gave equal weight to the three cultural tables, presumably to reflect the sovereignty of these Nations. Most of the representatives deferred to the expert panel (table 11) for the weights on the hypotheses, although several representatives chose either the high or the low end of the confidence bounds expressed by the experts.

Table 12. Objective weights.

[The weights derived from swing weighting for each of the measurable attributes are shown, for each agency and tribe in attendance at the second workshop. In addition, the weights across the three different cultural tables are shown for each agency, as well as the beliefs in the three hypotheses that characterized the key uncertainties. AZGF, Arizona Game and Fish Department; BoR, Bureau of Reclamation; FWS, Fish and Wildlife Service; NPS, National Park Service; WAPA, Western Area Power Administration; RBT, rainbow trout; HFE, high-flow experiment]

Objective	AZGF	BoR	FWS	Hopi	Navajo	NPS	WAPA	Zuni	Average
1A	0.029	0.067	0.036	0.105	0.039	0.046	0.047	0.093	0.058
1B	0.042	0.061	0.036	0.100	0.039	0.046	0.052	0.070	0.056
1C	0.038	0.020	0.035	0.084	0.043	0.048	0.058	0.075	0.050
1D	0.025	0.013	0.036	0.063	0.039	0.046	0.038	0.075	0.042
2A	0.125	0.147	0.098	0.211	0.099	0.110	0.186	0.134	0.139
2B1	0.037	0.018	0.027	0.014	0.038	0.028	0.023	0.039	0.028
2B2	0.061	0.036	0.032	0.023	0.023	0.020	0.020	0.039	0.032
2C1	0.025	0.015	0.026	0.012	0.031	0.025	0.021	0.039	0.024
2C2	0.055	0.007	0.029	0.022	0.015	0.020	0.014	0.039	0.025
2D1	0.089	0.105	0.171	0.004	0.161	0.116	0.026	0.078	0.094
2D2	0.075	0.044	0.093	0.105	0.079	0.122	0.074	0.100	0.087
3A1	0.091	0.032	0.040	0.009	0.016	0.033	0.047	0.008	0.034
3A2	0.054	0.020	0.042	0.088	0.019	0.049	0.055	0.008	0.042
3B	0.007	0.077	0.039	0.084	0.033	0.096	0.049	0.009	0.049
3C	0.015	0.046	0.037	0.004	0.056	0.067	0.029	0.007	0.033
3D	0.005	0.004	0.033	0.002	0.032	0.001	0.019	0.008	0.013
4A	0.073	0.040	0.038	0.007	0.022	0.033	0.047	0.008	0.033
4C	0.111	0.114	0.095	0.035	0.071	0.070	0.078	0.016	0.074
4E	0.013	0.078	0.038	0.005	0.075	0.004	0.065	0.104	0.048
4F	0.032	0.055	0.019	0.026	0.068	0.019	0.052	0.052	0.040
Weights on Cultural Tables:									
Zuni	0.8	1.0	1.0	1.0	1.0	1.0	1.0	1.0	1.0
Hopi	1.0	1.0	1.0	1.0	1.0	1.0	1.0	0.0	1.0
Navajo	1.0	1.0	1.0	1.0	1.0	0.0	1.0	0.0	1.0
Hypothesis Weights:									
RBT	0.653	0.653	0.653	0.463	0.653	0.500	0.780	0.653	0.653
Flow	0.600	0.713	0.713	0.713	0.713	0.500	0.822	0.713	0.713
HFE	0.400	0.500	0.500	0.250	0.500	0.500	0.715	0.500	0.500

There were some substantial differences in the assignment of weights on the objectives among representatives (table 12). A principal components analysis of the objective weights showed that 68.7 percent of the variation could be explained by the first two principal components (fig. 6). The first principal component was positively correlated with the weight on the cultural objectives (1A–1D) and the humpback chub objective (2A) and negatively correlated with the non-native fish objective (2D1). The second principal component was positively correlated with the sport fishery objectives (3A1, 3A2, 4A) and cost objective (4C) and negatively correlated with the power generation objective (4E). The plots of the scores for these components for each agency and Tribe help to show the diversity of views expressed through this process (fig. 6).

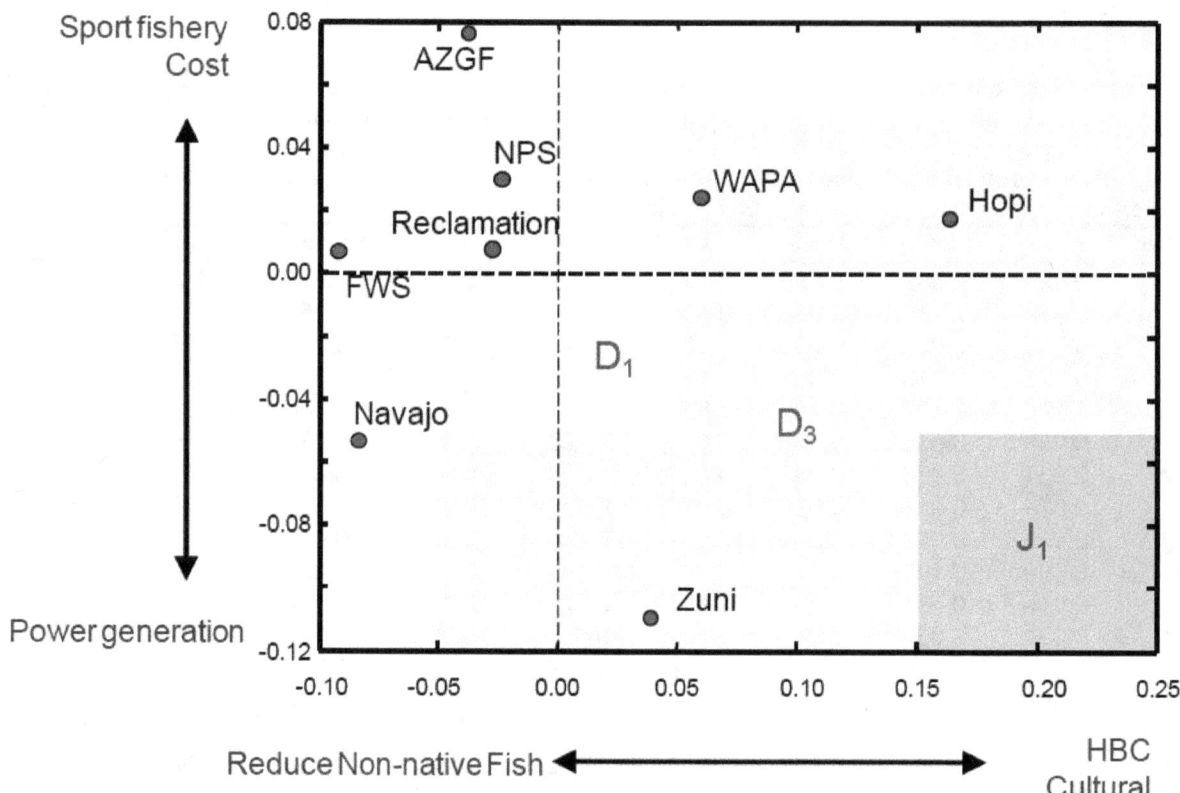

Figure 6. Graph showing principal-components analysis of the objective weights. The first principal component (which explains 47.4 percent of the variation in objective weights across the eight agencies and tribes) is driven positively by the weights on humpback chub recovery (2A) and the cultural objectives (1A–1D), and negatively by the weight on reducing non-native fish abundance in the Canyon (2D). The second principal component (which explains an additional 21.3 percent of the variation) is driven positively by the weights on the sport fishery (3A1, 3A1, 4A) and cost (4C) objectives, and negatively by the weight on the power generation objective (4E). The shaded regions of the graph show the hybrid portfolios (D_1, D_3, and J_1) favored under each combination of 1st and 2nd principal component (with the remaining principal components at their average values). The objectives are defined in table 1 and the hybrid portfolios are defined in table 3. AZGF, Arizona Game and Fish Department; NPS, National Park Service; WAPA, Western Area Power Administration; FWS, U.S. Fish and Wildlife Service; Reclamation, Bureau of Reclamation; HBC, humpback chub.

7.2. Analysis of Hybrid Portfolios in the Face of Uncertainty

The objective weights, cultural table weights, and hypothesis weights unique to each agency or Tribal representative were used as input to a multi-criteria decision analysis to produce individual rankings of the alternatives (table 13). All agencies and Tribes identified either D_1 or D_3 as their preferred alternative, and those two alternatives were found in the top three for every agency or Tribe. The only other alternatives to place in any representative's top two were A and J_1. Alternatives C_3 and K showed uniformly poor performance across objective weightings. When the objective weights were averaged across representatives, equal weights were given to the cultural tables, and the expert-derived hypothesis weights were used, the best-performing alternative was D_1.

Table 13. Composite scores from the multi-criteria decision analysis for each hybrid portfolio, using the objective and hypothesis weights of the individual agencies and Tribes.

[The pink shading shows the lowest ranking alternative for each Federal/State agency or Tribe, and the green shading shows the highest ranking. The top five alternatives are also shown. Yellow and light yellow shading are used to draw attention to hybrid portfolios D_1 and D_3, respectively. AZGF, Arizona Game and Fish Department; BoR, Bureau of Reclamation; FWS, Fish and Wildlife Service; NPS, National Park Service; WAPA, Western Area Power Administration]

Hybrid portfolio	AZGF	BoR	FWS	Hopi	Navajo	NPS	WAPA	Zuni	Average
A	0.598	0.527	0.497	0.563	0.498	0.647	0.432	0.462	0.501
C_2	0.505	0.418	0.418	0.450	0.428	0.474	0.308	0.314	0.402
C_3	0.427	0.380	0.373	0.419	0.397	0.443	0.280	0.267	0.361
C_4	0.478	0.440	0.428	0.545	0.458	0.512	0.353	0.370	0.437
C_5	0.444	0.404	0.397	0.527	0.433	0.483	0.326	0.366	0.411
D_1	0.672	0.589	0.649	0.571	0.648	0.629	0.557	0.504	0.606
D_2	0.584	0.538	0.596	0.525	0.610	0.598	0.519	0.457	0.554
D_3	0.610	0.578	0.623	0.618	0.645	0.651	0.565	0.558	0.603
J_1	0.522	0.496	0.567	0.586	0.553	0.503	0.501	0.519	0.539
J_1'	0.610	0.525	0.583	0.528	0.537	0.508	0.523	0.481	0.545
J_2	0.439	0.452	0.519	0.559	0.522	0.474	0.472	0.471	0.497
J_2'	0.524	0.479	0.532	0.497	0.503	0.473	0.491	0.433	0.500
K	0.365	0.387	0.426	0.459	0.436	0.472	0.293	0.346	0.390

Rank									
1	D_1	D_1	D_1	D_3	D_1	D_3	D_3	D_3	D_1
2	J_1'	D_3	D_3	J_1	D_3	A	D_1	J_1	D_3
3	D_3	D_2	D_2	D_1	D_2	D_1	J_1'	D_1	D_2
4	A	A	J_1'	A	J_1	D_2	D_2	J_1'	J_1'
5	D_2	J_1'	J_1	J_2	J_1'	C_4	J_1	J_2	J_1

To explore the sensitivity of the best-performing alternative to the weights on the objectives, the best-performing alternative was calculated over a grid of values from the first two principal components (fig. 6); the patterns help to explain the difference in preference among representatives. Alternative D_1 is favored at the average objective weights, and continued to be favored as more weight is given to sport fishery objectives, cost objective, or the desire to reduce non-native fish in the ecosystem. As more weight is given to cultural objectives or humpback chub objectives, D_3 is favored. At strong weightings of cultural objectives and power generation, J_1 rises to the top. It's worth noting that figure 6 only shows the effect of the first two principal components. The NPS weighting for the first two components indicates that D_1 is their best-performing alternative, but in fact it is D_3 because of weight given to the native fish and recreational objectives (which appear in the third principal component). The result, however, is that the ranking of alternatives D_1 and D_3 is fairly robust to variation in the objective weights.

7.3. Value of Information

The results presented in the previous section reflect the ranking of the alternatives in the face of uncertainty. Throughout the development of this analysis, there was substantial discussion among the participants about the importance of uncertainty, with the implication that the resolution of uncertainty might lead to different preferred non-native fish control strategies. Value of information methods from the field of decision analysis (Runge and others, in press) provide a way of assessing the importance of uncertainty in a decision context. These methods are different from typical sensitivity analyses—they do not just determine whether there is substantial uncertainty in the system dynamics, but whether that uncertainty would change the decision.

Uncertainty was compared across the three hypotheses the expert panel had evaluated, by constructing eight scenarios that included all permutations of those hypotheses, then conducting a value of information analysis (table 14) using the average weights on the objectives. It was assumed that the hypotheses were independent, so that the probability of each combination could be calculated from the appropriate product of beliefs in each of the component hypotheses.

Table 14. Expected value of perfect information for discerning among the underlying hypotheses.

[The composite score from the multi-criteria decision analysis, using the average objective weights, is shown for each of eight combinations of the three underlying hypotheses (the HFE, RBT, and Flow hypotheses). The green shading shows the preferred alternative under each combination of hypotheses. In the face of uncertainty, the average response weighted across hypotheses indicates that D_1 is the best action to take, with composite score of 0.606. If uncertainty can be fully resolved before choosing an action, the expected performance increases to 0.643 (light green shading). Thus the expected value of perfect information is 0.038 (6.2 percent increase over the expected response in the face of uncertainty). HFE, high-flow experiment; RBT, rainbow trout]

	Eight combinations of the underlying hypotheses								Average
HFE	No	No	No	No	Yes	Yes	Yes	Yes	
RBT	No	No	Yes	Yes	No	No	Yes	Yes	
Flow	No	Yes	No	Yes	No	Yes	No	Yes	
Weight	0.050	0.124	0.094	0.233	0.050	0.124	0.094	0.233	
Alternative									
A	0.875	0.875	0.391	0.391	0.766	0.766	0.271	0.271	0.501
C_2	0.700	0.700	0.451	0.451	0.590	0.590	0.095	0.095	0.402
C_3	0.659	0.659	0.410	0.410	0.549	0.549	0.053	0.053	0.361
C_4	0.735	0.735	0.486	0.486	0.624	0.624	0.129	0.129	0.437
C_5	0.709	0.709	0.460	0.460	0.598	0.598	0.103	0.103	0.411
D_1	0.716	0.716	0.589	0.589	0.708	0.708	0.509	0.509	0.606
D_2	0.665	0.665	0.538	0.538	0.657	0.657	0.458	0.458	0.555
D_3	0.713	0.713	0.587	0.587	0.705	0.705	0.506	0.506	0.603
J_1	0.630	0.631	0.504	0.513	0.622	0.629	0.423	0.491	0.539
J_1'	0.646	0.646	0.506	0.517	0.638	0.644	0.426	0.492	0.546
J_2	0.589	0.589	0.462	0.472	0.581	0.587	0.382	0.450	0.497
J_2'	0.601	0.601	0.461	0.472	0.593	0.599	0.381	0.447	0.501
K	0.674	0.674	0.250	0.258	0.665	0.667	0.205	0.237	0.390
Best	0.875	0.875	0.589	0.589	0.766	0.766	0.509	0.509	0.643

The best performing alternative in the face of uncertainty, that is, averaged over the eight scenarios, is D_1 (as noted in section 7.2), but if uncertainty could be fully removed before committing to an action, there are scenarios that point to Portfolio A as the best-performing alternative. If the uncertainty can be removed before an action is taken, the expected performance increases from 0.608 to 0.645, thus, the expected value of perfect information (EVPI) across these hypotheses is 0.038 (or a 6.2-percent increase in performance). But note that all of this value of information comes from resolving uncertainty about the RBT hypothesis, and none from resolving uncertainty about the HFE or Flow hypotheses. The partial value of perfect information is 6.2 percent for the RBT hypothesis, and 0 percent for the HFE and Flow hypotheses. This is not to say there isn't uncertainty about the HFE and Flow hypotheses—the experts agreed that there was—just that it does not affect the top-ranked alternative.

The uncertainty in the other hypotheses does have some subtle effects, however, on the second-to fifth-ranking portfolios (fig. 7). In particular, even if rainbow trout do not threaten chub, an HFE effect increases the ranking of upstream removal portfolios (like D_1, and D_3) to reduce the number of non-native fish in the river ecosystem.

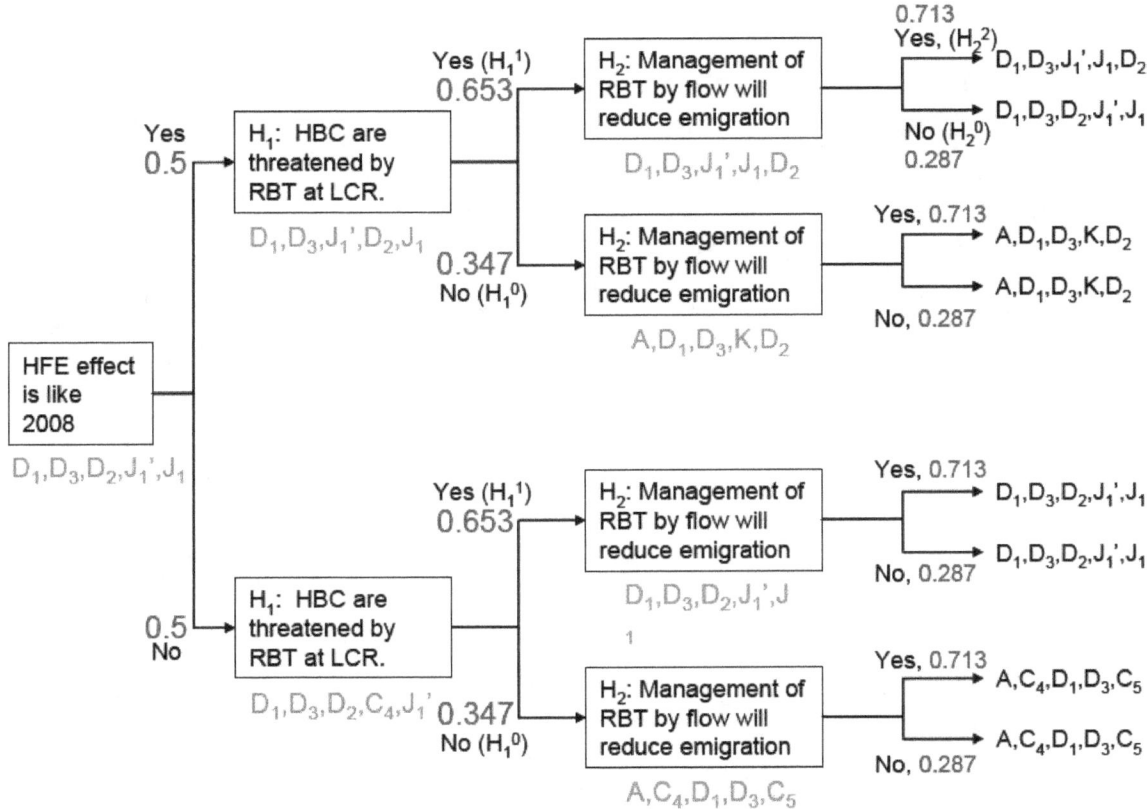

Figure 7. Flowchart showing the preferred alternatives as a function of the underlying hypotheses. The final nodes at the right of the tree show the top-ranked alternatives (in decreasing order) if the uncertainty can be fully resolved on all three hypotheses. For example, if all three hypotheses are true, then the preferred alternative is D_1 followed by D_3. The next node back shows the top-ranked alternatives averaged over the flow hypothesis (using the mean expert weight). The first node on the left shows the top-ranked alternatives in the face of uncertainty about all three hypotheses (using the mean expert weights). The weights on each hypothesis, based on expert judgment (table 11), are shown in blue at each node. The hybrid portfolios (A, C_4, D_1, and others) are defined in table 3.

The analysis shows that Portfolio A is favored whenever the RBT hypothesis is false, and Portfolio D_1 is favored whenever the RBT hypothesis is true. If the RBT hypothesis is false, humpback chub are not threatened by rainbow trout, and there is no need to undertake removals. The other objectives push the strategy toward no action. If the RBT hypothesis is true, the humpback chub objective (on which all representatives placed substantial weight) has the most influence, and trout removal in the PBR of Upper Marble Canyon is favored. The preferred portfolio switches from A to D_1 as a function of the weight on the RBT hypothesis (fig. 8). If the weight on the RBT hypothesis is less than 0.33, the best performing portfolio is A, otherwise it is D_1 (with D_3 an extremely close second). The expert panel believed the evidence provided 0.653 weight on the RBT hypothesis, with an 80-percent confidence interval that did not include 0.33, indicating that the choice of Portfolio D_1 over A is robust to the level of uncertainty about the RBT hypothesis.

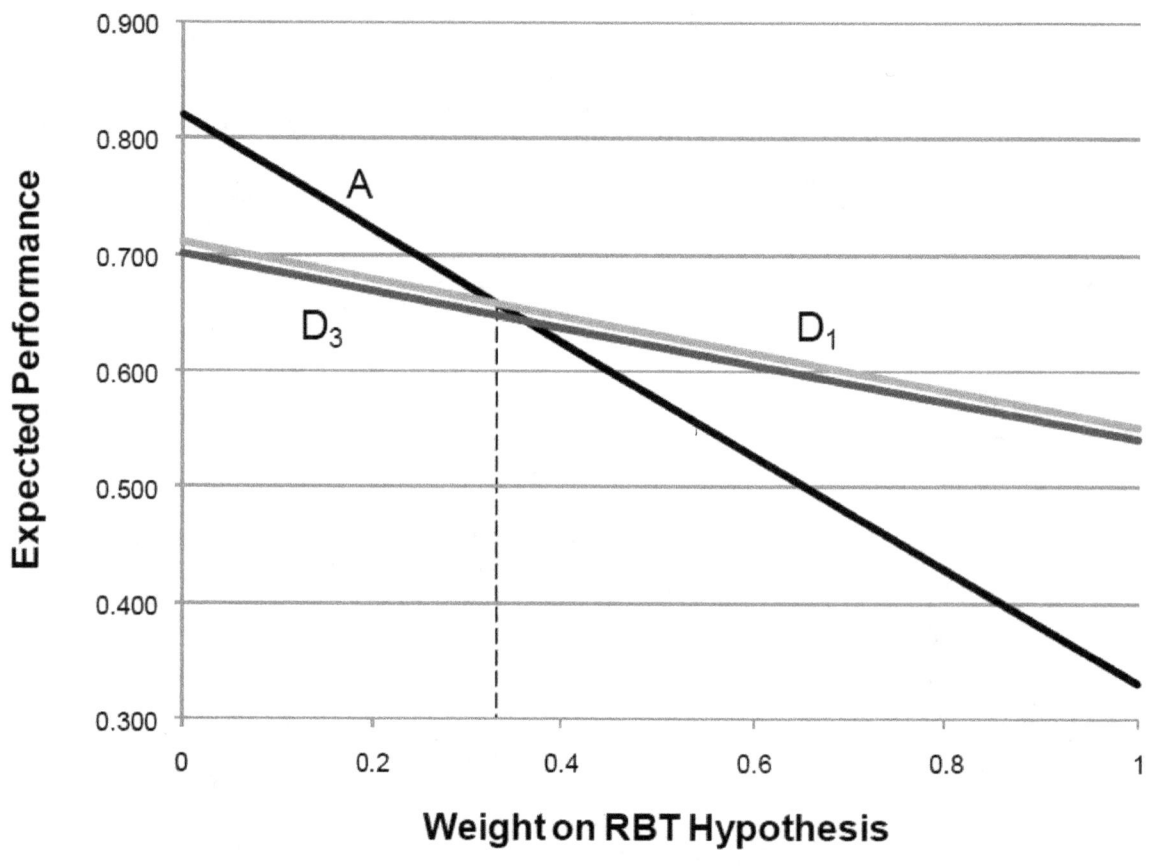

Figure 8. Graph showing expected performance of three hybrid portfolios as a function of the weight on the rainbow trout (RBT) hypothesis. If the weight on the RBT hypothesis is less than 0.33, alternative A (no action) is preferred; otherwise D_1 (removal curtain) is preferred. Note that with the average objective weights, alternative D_3 slightly underperforms D_1 across all weights on the RBT hypothesis.

7.4. Adaptive Strategies

Adaptive strategies are designed to resolve uncertainty passively over time by allowing monitoring to provide feedback about the underlying hypotheses, and actively by undertaking probing actions designed to accelerate learning. But adaptive strategies are only valuable if they target uncertainty for which there is a high value of information, that is, uncertainty that leads to different preferred actions. The results of the EVPI analysis indicate there is some value in resolving the RBT hypothesis, but not much (only 6.2 percent expected increase in performance) because the evidence already favors D_1 strongly. Further, the results indicate that the other hypotheses are not worth testing, at least for the decision regarding non-native fish control. By this argument, an effective adaptive strategy might be characterized as {A, D}, a strategy that uses either Portfolios A or D in the long-run, and seeks to resolve uncertainty about the RBT hypothesis in the short-run. There is little in this analysis to indicate that a more complicated adaptive strategy is needed, at least with regard to the non-native fish control decision.

The removal curtain portfolios (the variants of D) already have an implicit adaptive component because they include removal at both LCR and PBR. That is, D is already an adaptive strategy that combines C (a pure LCR removal portfolio) with a pure PBR removal portfolio. The LCR removal component provides assurance that if the PBR removal is impractical or ineffective, there is a back-up plan for removing trout in the Canyon downstream where humpback chub exist. Thus, an adaptive strategy that combines {A, C, D} addresses both the uncertainty about the effect of rainbow trout on humpback chub, as well as uncertainty about the effectiveness of PBR removal (which was not specifically evaluated in this analysis).

Other adaptive strategies have been proposed in 2010, both formally and informally, by a number of groups. The "kitchen sink" proposal, as originally described by Richard Valdez and others (written commun., 2010), was an experimental strategy that combined a large number of potential management actions and sought to first implement them all, then remove them piecemeal to find a cost-effective strategy. The "adaptive control" proposal, by Mike Senn and others (AZGF, written commun., 2010), is a more refined adaptive strategy that might be characterized as {C, D, J}, and focuses on resolving uncertainty in two ways: (1) whether PBR removal can be successful in reducing downstream emigration, and (2) whether various flow regimes can be effective in reducing rainbow trout production and emigration from the Lees Ferry reach. The analysis in this report, however, does not naturally lead to inclusion of flow regimes in an adaptive strategy because flow regimes are not superior to PBR removal under any of the scenarios investigated. It is worth asking if something was left out of the analysis that would favor flow regimes. First, uncertainty about the effectiveness of PBR removal was not specifically investigated. If PBR removal is not effective, flow regimes may become more advantageous. Second, the cost and effort of PBR removal is thought to be quite high, whereas flow regimes themselves have minimal cost and might possibly increase power revenue. It is possible costs in this analysis were not weighed properly. Third, cultural values may favor flow regimes over PBR removal in ways that the analysis in this report did not fully capture. Several Tribal representatives have indicated that non-native fish control that more closely mimics natural processes (like flow manipulations) would be preferable and more in line with cultural values than more aggressive human-mediated control (like removal). Because the kitchen sink portfolios (J_1, and others) included LCR and PBR removal, they did not have high scores on cultural attributes. A pure flow portfolio (for example, like J_1 but without the removal actions) might have scored much higher on cultural objectives than the kitchen sink portfolios, and might be favored as the preferred portfolio if the weight on the RBT and flow hypotheses were strong. Thus, our alternatives and scoring may need to be restructured to examine the value of a long-term strategy that relies primarily on flow manipulations.

8. Summary and Discussion

The purpose of this report is to describe the methods used to provide a structured forum in which cooperating agencies and Tribes could provide substantive input to Reclamation regarding methods and necessity of controlling non-native fish in the Colorado River ecosystem below Glen Canyon Dam. The intent of the forum was not to reach a consensus recommendation, nor provide a single preferred alternative to Reclamation, but rather to understand the values that were important to the stakeholders and relevant to controlling non-native fish populations.

A broad array of decision-making objectives was identified and defined, and an effort was made to understand how these objectives are likely to be achieved by a variety of strategies. A set of alternative approaches was developed, and the complex structure of those alternatives was illustrated. Multi-criteria decision-analysis methods allowed the evaluation of those alternatives against the array of objectives, while preserving the values of individual agencies and Tribes.

Trout removal strategies aimed at the PBR, with a variety of permutations in deference to Tribal cultural values, were identified as top-ranking options for all agencies and Tribes. These PBR removal approaches outperformed LCR removal approaches, both for cultural and effectiveness reasons—the probability of keeping the humpback chub population above 6,000 was estimated to be higher under the PBR portfolios than under the LCR-only portfolios (tables 5, 7). The PBR removal portfolios also outperformed portfolios based on flow manipulations, primarily because of the effect of sport fishery, wilderness recreation, and cultural objectives. The preference for the PBR removal portfolios (particularly D_1 and D_3) was dominant despite variation in the objective weights and uncertainty about the underlying dynamics, at least over the ranges investigated in this round of structured decision making on the topic of non-native fish control.

A value of information analysis pointed to an adaptive strategy that contemplates three possible long-term management actions (no action, A; LCR removal, C; or PBR removal, D) and seeks to reduce uncertainty about the following two issues: the degree to which rainbow trout limit humpback chub populations, and the effectiveness of PBR removal to reduce trout emigration downstream in the Marble and Grand Canyons. By bringing in considerations not captured in this analysis, a case might be made for including flow manipulations in an adaptive strategy, but we emphasize that the analysis herein does not lead to that conclusion.

The decision analysis described in this report is meant to aid Reclamation by helping them see the central structure of the non-native fish control decision, but is not meant to make the decision for them. This analysis can best be used as a structure and starting point for the deliberative consultations that will lead to the final decision as the EA process proceeds to completion.

8.1. Disagreement about the Science

Differing opinions on key uncertainties, such as the hypothesis about the effect of rainbow trout on humpback chub, were acting as partial impediments to decision making. Prior to the SDM workshops, participants voiced a wide range of beliefs ranging from near dismissal of any effect of rainbow trout on humpback chub to near certainty of that effect. During the second workshop, scientists presented current evidence and expressed their judgments regarding the strength of evidence for the key uncertainties. At the end of the second workshop, each agency and Tribe was given the opportunity to express their belief about the weight of evidence for these key hypotheses. In general, the range of opinions narrowed. Also, the differences in opinions on key uncertainties did not determine the preferred portfolios, and thus should not impede decision making.

As part of this process, an age-structured population model was built by subject matter experts to aid in decision making. The model, while rapidly developed, reflects current scientific understanding about ecological relationships and the population dynamics of humpback chub in the Colorado and Little Colorado Rivers. This predictive population model allowed (1) assumptions to be fully identified and tested, (2) sensitivity of the decision to sources of uncertainties to be evaluated, and (3) current status of knowledge to be communicated to facilitate a common understanding of the scientific basis for management. Further, the model is a valuable starting point, which can be updated and revised as information improves and learning continues to occur in the GCDAMP.

8.2. Cultural Values and the Viewpoint of the Tribes

The assessment of the consequences of alternative non-native fish control strategies on cultural objectives was limited in scope and not necessarily representative of the appropriate persons or decision making bodies within the Tribes. As such, the scores shown in table 4 are not fully representative of the actual preferences and values, but were included as place holders for the Tribal perspectives. If further input is required from the Tribes, additional consultation could occur at the government-to-government level and could, at a minimum, include discussion of the topics listed toward the end of this section, as well as the potential consequences of the proposed actions on the objectives. The Tribal representatives suggested that succinct summaries of each of the following would be valuable when consulting with the Tribes: (1) the main scientific evidence in support of removing trout, (2) the potential "footprint" of each of the proposed actions, and (3) the beneficial effects of the proposed actions on the humpback chub population. The description of the footprint would include location, duration, and frequency of the activity; the targeted species, including numbers of individuals affected; numbers of staff involved, and equipment being considered; proposed use of any fish removed; and cost.

It was challenging to elicit and define cultural and spiritual values. The decision analysis process required participants to deconstruct the elements of the decision and to evaluate individual objectives against the hybrid portfolios. In other words, objectives were taken in isolation and consequences evaluated; tradeoffs among the whole suite of objectives were considered in the final analysis, but this step was not readily apparent from the initial scoring of the consequence matrix. In the language of decision analysis, the assumption of preferential independence did not hold for cultural objectives. Thus, this approach was unsatisfactory for some of the Tribal representatives, because the relative appropriateness of any particular portfolio depended on the context of the action being applied. For example, the taking of life may be appropriate provided it serves a greater purpose, namely to sustain other life. Yet considered in isolation that objective scored poorly in the consequence matrix as the relative context was not clearly defined. Because of the difficulty this framework posed for defining and scoring cultural objectives, the importance of cultural objectives to the selection of top portfolios might not be appropriately captured in this analysis.

As noted in the previous paragraph, several questions were highlighted by the Tribal representatives. These include:

1. What is the evidence for stating that rainbow trout are negatively affecting humpback chub persistence and recruitment? To what degree is the science certain about this hypothesis?

2. If rainbow trout are having a negative effect, what are the long-term solutions for reducing emigration and threats from predation and competition? Repeated removal activities are likely infeasible over the long term, and will not sufficiently address cultural concerns.

3. Can the problem be thought of more holistically? For example, rather than focus on a certain number of rainbow trout, would it be useful to think about the ratio between trout and humpback chub and how that ratio may temper interactions?

4. What about the other non-native species in the system? That is, why is the issue focused only on the trout?

Finally, throughout this project, there was considerable discussion about the process by which Reclamation was making its decision. Of particular concern was the extent to which Tribal values were going to be incorporated in the decision making, and the need for direct government-to-government consultation. While it was not the purpose of this project to negotiate the timing and substance of such consultation, it is understood that the tribes are still interested in direct conversation with Reclamation and DOI on this issue. This report may provide a structure that could help to organize those ongoing consultations.

8.3. High-Flow Experimental Dam Releases (HFE)

In a parallel NEPA process, Reclamation is developing an EA regarding a protocol for repeated HFE releases from Glen Canyon Dam for the purpose of determining whether or not there is sufficient remaining renewable sand supply from tributaries below the dam to rebuild and maintain sandbar habitats throughout the Canyon (Wright and others, 2008; Rubin and others, 2002). As the consequence analysis in this report indicates, there is a close relation between the HFE decision and the non-native fish control decision, because of the apparent effect that HFEs have on increasing rainbow trout recruitment in the Lees Ferry tailwaters reach. The coupled trout-chub models developed as part of this report provide some valuable predictions about the effects of HFEs (table 7). If rainbow trout are indeed limiting humpback chub, then repeated ongoing high-flows may reduce the likelihood of keeping humpback chub population levels in the desired range. Aggressive rainbow trout removal at PBR, coupled with back-up removal at LCR (i.e., Portfolio D_1 or D_3), and perhaps with trout-suppression flows (i.e., Portfolio J), provides the best opportunity for mitigating the potentially harmful effects of more frequent HFEs on the LCR chub population. Such an investigation was not the primary purpose of the analysis in this report, but the models described in this report (Lew Coggins, Service, and Josh Korman, Ecometric Research, Inc., written commun., 2010) may be valuable in the future for evaluating the effect of HFEs.

8.4. Linked Decisions

In this decision analysis, the question of non-native fish control was treated as an isolated decision, but as the preceding section discusses, non-native fish control is linked to decisions about high-flow experiments, and likely to other decisions as well. When linked decisions are analyzed separately, the independent results may work against each other or at least may not be optimal. On the other hand, the combined problem may be fairly difficult to solve, especially if the time-frame, jurisdiction, and stakeholder interests differ for the linked pieces. One way around this problem is to include objectives that acknowledge the linkage between the two decision contexts. Two objectives and one hypothesis in this decision analysis acknowledge the link between the HFE and the non-native fish EAs: Objective 5C (support HFE EA) seeks a non-native fish control solution that does not undermine the HFE protocol; Objective 4C (minimize cost) recognizes that there are limited funds for operations and research; and the uncertainty around the HFE hypothesis builds in the rainbow trout response that might result from an HFE protocol.

The cost objective (Objective 4C) actually serves to indirectly link this decision to many other decisions. There is a limited amount of money available for operations, control, and research. By seeking to minimize the cost of non-native fish control, funds are available for other activities. But without defining the specific competing demands for funding, the participants in this process may have undervalued the cost objective.

The solution to the challenges brought about by linked decisions is to view the results in this report as an initial analysis, without consideration of linkages. These results of this report can be examined by Reclamation, DOI, and the GCDAMP, to consider the relation between the non-native fish control decision and other decisions (the HFE protocol among them).

8.5. Learning as a Means Objective

Throughout this SDM process, there was a strong interest on the part of many participants to advance solutions that focused heavily on learning. For example, adaptive strategies were recommended early on before uncertainty was defined, and learning was proposed as a fundamental objective. The decision analysts who facilitated the SDM process actively resisted this direction because Reclamation's decision was a management decision, not an academic decision. The role of learning in a management decision-making process is to reduce uncertainty that impedes decisions. Not all uncertainty impedes decisions, therefore, not all adaptive strategies are warranted. To identify adaptive strategies, the decision in the face of uncertainty must first be analyzed, then the value of information in improving expected performance must be evaluated. The value of information points toward useful adaptive, learning-centered strategies. In other words, learning is a means objective, not a fundamental objective.

The GCDAMP is centered on a mission of adaptive management, and so it is understandable that learning figures heavily in its planning. As outsiders to the GCDAMP, the authors of this report are not familiar with the history or objectives of the program, and do not know whether learning is appropriately a fundamental or means objective. If it is the latter, however, then decision analysis must precede experimental design. It is the decision context and the role of uncertainty that provide the justification for learning.

9. Acknowledgments

The authors thank Ann Gold and Glen Knowles from Reclamation for their generous help in explaining the framework for the non-native fish control decision. Gratitude is also given to the staff at the USGS Grand Canyon Monitoring and Research Center, especially Ted Melis, Matthew Andersen, John Hamill, and Kyrie Fry, who provided all the logistical arrangements for the SDM workshops. This project could not have been completed without the extraordinary contributions of the expert panels who worked between the two workshops to predict the consequences of the hybrid portfolios. Lew Coggins (Service) and Josh Korman (Ecometric Research, Inc.) deserve special recognition for developing the humpback chub and rainbow trout models, a challenging task that was completed in just 2 weeks. Other experts who made important contributions included: Jan Balsom (NPS); Helen Fairley, Ted Melis, and Mike Yard (GCMRC); Loretta Jackson-Kelly (Hualapai Tribe); Glen Knowles (Reclamation); Clayton Palmer (WAPA); Larry Riley and Bill Stewart (AZGF); and Mike Yeatts (Hopi Tribe). Glen Knowles, Ted Melis, Sam Spiller, Pam Sponholtz, and Drew Tyre provided careful reviews of, and editorial suggestions for, this report. Finally, for their open minds, generosity of spirit, and thoughtful contributions, the authors are grateful to the participants in the SDM workshops: Matthew Andersen, Helen Fairley, John Hamill, Ted Melis, and Mike Yard (GCMRC); Jan Balsom, Martha Hahn, Norm Henderson, and Palma Wilson (NPS); David Bennion, Shane Capron, LaVerne Kyriss, and Clayton Palmer (WAPA); Debra Bills, Lew Coggins, Sam Spiller, and Pam Sponholtz (Service); Charley Bulletts (Southern Paiute Consortium); Gary Cantley (BIA); Marianne Crawford, Ann Gold, Glen Knowles, Heather Patno, and David Trueman (Reclamation); Kurt Dongoske (Pueblo of Zuni); John Halliday, Rod Smith, and Justin Tade (DOI); John Jordan (Federation of Fly Fishers); Josh Korman (Ecometric Research, Inc.); Andy Makinster, Larry Riley, Mike Senn, and Bill Stewart (AZGF); James Morel (Navajo Nation); and Mike Yeatts (Hopi Tribe). Although this report attempts to reflect their expertise and values, this report does not express the official position of the participants or the agencies and Tribes they represent.

10. References Cited

Coggins, L.G., Jr., 2008, Active adaptive management for native fish management in the Grand Canyon—Implementation and evaluation: Gainesville, University of Florida, Ph.D. dissertation, 173 p.

Coggins, L.G., Jr., and Walters, C.J., 2009, Abundance trends and status of the Little Colorado River population of humpback chub; an update considering data from 1989–2008: U.S. Geological Survey Open-File Report 2009–1075, 18 p.

Coggins, L.G., Jr., and Yard, M.D., 2010, Mechanical removal of non-native fish in the Colorado River within Grand Canyon, in Melis, T.S., Hamill, J.F., Coggins, L.G., Bennett, G.E., Grams, P.E., Kennedy, T.A., Kubly, D.M., and Ralston, B.E., eds., Proceedings of the Colorado River Basin Science and Resource Management Symposium, November 18–20, 2008, Scottsdale, Arizona: U.S. Geological Survey Scientific Investigations Report 2010–5135, p. 227–234.

Coggins, L.G., Jr., Yard, M.D., and Pine, W.E., in press, Non-native fish control in the Colorado River in Grand Canyon, Arizona: an effective program or serendipitous timing? Transactions of the American Fisheries Society.

Cross, W.F., Rosi-Marshall, E.J., Behn, K.E., Kennedy, T.A., Hall, R.O., Jr., Fuller, A.E., and Baxter, C.V., 2010, Invasion and production of New Zealand mud snails in the Colorado River, Glen Canyon, Biological Invasions, DOI 10.1007/s10530-010-9694-y.

Hammond, J.S., Keeney, R.L., and Raiffa, H., 1999, Smart Choices: A Practical Guide to Making Better Life Decisions: New York, Broadway Books, 256 p.

Keeney, R.L., 2007, Developing objectives and attributes, in Edwards, W., Miles, R.F.J., and Von Winterfeldt, D., eds., Advances in decision analysis: from foundations to applications: Cambridge, UK, Cambridge University Press, p. 104–128.

Korman, J., 2009, Early life history dynamics of rainbow trout in a large regulated river: Vancouver, University of British Columbia, Ph.D. thesis, 214 p.

Korman, J., Kaplinski, M, and Melis, T.S., 2010, Effects of high-flow experiments from Glen Canyon Dam on abundance, growth, and survival rates of early life stages of rainbow trout in the Lees Ferry reach of the Colorado River: U.S. Geological Survey Open-File Report 2010–1034, 31 p.

Korman, J., Kaplinski, M., and Melis, T.S., in press, Effects of fluctuation flows and a controlled flood on incubation success and early survival rates and growth of age-0 rainbow trout in a large regulated river: Transactions of the American Fisheries Society.

Kuhnert, P.M., Martin, T.G., and Griffiths, S.P., 2010, A guide to eliciting and using expert knowledge in Bayesian ecological models, Ecology Letters, v. 13, p. 900–914.

Makinster, A.S., Persons, W.R., Avery, L.A., and Bunch, A.J., 2010, Colorado River fish monitoring in Grand Canyon, Arizona—2000 to 2009 summary: U.S. Geological Survey Open-File Report 2010–1246, 26 p.

McKinney, T., and Persons, W.R., 1999, Rainbow trout and lower tropic levels in the Lees Ferry tailwater below Glen Canyon Dam, Arizona—a review: Phoenix, Arizona Fish and Game Department, 53 p.

National Park Service, 2006, Management Policies: Washington, DC, National Park Service, U.S. Department of the Interior, 180 p.

Randle, T.J., Lyons, J.K., Christensen, R.J., and Stephen, R.D., 2007, Colorado River ecosystem sediment augmentation appraisal engineering report, Bureau of Reclamation, 71 p.

Rubin, D.M., Topping, D.J., Schmidt, J.C., Hazel, J., Kaplinski, M., and Melis, T.S., 2002, Recent sediment studies refute Glen Canyon Dam hypothesis: Eos, Transactions of the American Geophysical Union, v. 83, no. 25, p. 273, 277–278.

Runge, M.C., Converse, S.J., and Lyons, J.E., in press, Which uncertainty? Using expert elicitation and expected value of information to design an adaptive program, Biological Conservation.

Silberman, J., 2003, The economic importance of fishing and hunting: economic data on fishing and hunting for the State of Arizona and for each Arizona County, Report to the Arizona Game and Fish Department: Phoenix, School of Management, Arizona State University West, 98 p.

Speirs-Bridge, A., Fidler, F., McBride, M.F., Flander, L., Cumming, G., and Burgman, M.A., 2010, Reducing overconfidence in the interval judgments of experts, Risk Analysis, v. 30, p. 512–523.

U.S. Department of the Interior, 1996, Record of Decision, Operation of Glen Canyon Dam Final Environmental Impact Statement: Washington, DC, Office of the Secretary of the Interior, 15 p.

von Winterfeldt, D., and Edwards, W., 1986, Decision analysis and behavioral research: Cambridge, UK, Cambridge University Press, 624 p.

Wright, S.A., Schmidt, J.C., Melis, T.S., Topping, D.J., and Rubin, D.M., 2008, Is there enough sand? Evaluating the fate of Grand Canyon sandbars: Geological Society of America Today, v. 18, no. 8, p. 4–10.

Yard, M.D., Coggins, L.G., Baxter, C.V., and Bennett, G.E., in press, Trout piscivory in the Colorado River, Grand Canyon—effects of turbidity, temperature, and fish prey availability: Transactions of the American Fisheries Society.

Appendix 1 Letter from Anne Castle to Adaptive Management Working Group and Technical Working Group Members and Alternates, September 17, 2010

TO: AMWG AND TWG MEMBERS AND ALTERNATES

FROM: ANNE CASTLE, SECRETARY'S DESIGNEE, ASSISTANT SECRETARY FOR WATER AND SCIENCE

DATE: SEPTEMBER 17, 2010

SUBJECT: ENVIRONMENTAL ASSESSMENT OF METHODS OF NON-NATIVE FISH CONTROL

The Bureau of Reclamation (Reclamation) has been engaged for several months in an Environmental Assessment (EA) of various methods of controlling non-native fish in the Grand Canyon. Because nonnative fish, particularly rainbow and brown trout, are known to prey on the endangered humpback chub, the U.S. Fish and Wildlife Service (FWS) 2008 Biological Opinion included a conservation measure that addressed non-native fish control. That conservation measure provided that Reclamation would continue non-native control efforts through the Adaptive Management Program (AMP) and anticipated the mechanical removal of non-native trout at the confluence of the Colorado River mainstem and the Little Colorado River (LCR), as well as other control methods. Grave concern has been expressed by several of the Native American tribes that are represented on the Adaptive Management Work Group (AMWG), particularly the Pueblo of Zuni, about this taking of life within a place that is sacred to the tribes and fundamental in several creation stories.

In direct response to these concerns, Reclamation determined to forego the planned mechanical removal trips during 2010 and to take time to evaluate alternative methods of non-native fish control in upcoming years. Reclamation re-initiated consultation with FWS on the planned delay and FWS agreed to review the one-year hiatus in the use of mechanical removal. In early 2010, Reclamation initiated an EA process to evaluate non-native fish control alternatives. The Pueblo of Zuni, the Hualapai tribe, U.S. Geological Survey (USGS), Bureau of Indian Affairs, FWS, National Park Service, Arizona Game and Fish Department, and Western Area Power Administration are cooperating agencies to Reclamation in the EA process. Thus far, several meetings and conference calls have occurred with the cooperating agencies and interested members of the public. The cooperating agencies continue to participate on weekly conference calls. Formal, government-to-government consultation with the interested and affected Native American tribes and pueblos is ongoing. These ongoing efforts as part of the AMP were discussed with AMWG members and other stakeholders at last month's AMWG meeting in Phoenix.

This is an issue that requires extremely careful evaluation. As a federal agency, Reclamation is required to ensure that its actions do not jeopardize the continued existence of endangered species, in this case, the humpback chub in particular. Trout have been identified as a known predator of young humpback chub, particularly in the area of the confluence of the Colorado River and the LCR, and mechanical removal of trout at that location through the AMP has been specified as a conservation measure in the FWS's 2008 Biological Opinion. At the same time, various tribes have objected to the taking of life through the mechanical removal process and particularly at the confluence. Reclamation is also obligated to conduct government-to-government consultation with the tribes and pueblos on matters of concern, a process that does not pre-determine the outcome of any such discussions but requires that meaningful and timely tribal input is secured. Such consultation ensures that our officials have the input and recommendations of the tribes and pueblos, and that such input is fully considered by Departmental officials. We remain committed to meaningful government-to-government consultation in this process.

Our goal in the EA process is to promote: (a) the best possible engagement of all interested parties, including the AMWG members and other stakeholders; (b) appropriate and adequate opportunity by all parties to express their views, and; (c) meaningful participation by all parties in the process of proposing and evaluating alternative non-native fish control measures that will serve to implement the non-native control conservation measure and assist in the conservation of the endangered native fish. To that end, I have requested that Reclamation utilize a Structured Decision Making (SDM) process to evaluate options for non-native fish control. In the SDM process, the discussions of alternatives will be guided by an experienced facilitator who is knowledgeable about the constraints imposed by law on Reclamation for protection of the humpback chub, but also cognizant of the gravity of the concerns expressed about the mechanical removal method. Dr. Michael C. Runge, Research Ecologist from the USGS Patuxent Wildlife Research Center, an expert in the use of SDM, will facilitate two 2½-day workshops in Phoenix in October or November, through which the cooperating agencies will work to develop, evaluate, and assess alternatives for consideration in the EA.

This type of process has not been widely used in environmental assessment processes, but the disparate interests involved here and the need to work within applicable legal constraints have led me to conclude that SDM may serve our purposes well and we should give it a try. While we are eager to utilize and assess the effectiveness of SDM in this effort, I want to emphasize that this process will entail "structured" decision-making, but not "delegated" decision-making. The federal agencies involved here cannot delegate or abdicate their statutory responsibilities and do not intend to do so. Nevertheless, we believe that through the involvement and participation by all stakeholders, operating within the framework of our legal obligations, we can reach a more-informed, effective, and implementable set of final agency decisions. Whatever the outcome of the alternatives evaluated and the preferred alternative selected, I am hopeful that the SDM process will ensure that all voices have been fully heard and that appropriate accommodations are made when feasible.

As described, the use of the SDM method involves concentrated and dedicated time and effort by multiple parties. In order to schedule the two recommended workshops and ensure strong participation by interested stakeholders, the schedule we initially set out for completion of this EA must be extended. We now expect that Reclamation will complete the EA by December 8, 2010, and the FWS will render a new Biological Opinion on the preferred alternative no later than April 23, 2011. I realize that this delay is not ideal, but I am convinced that it is advisable in order to fully engage the wide-ranging interests at stake. This revised schedule will not undermine Reclamation's ability to conduct any necessary nonnative fish control during appropriate periods in 2011.

Appendix 2 Detailed Description of the Hybrid Portfolios

Abbreviations Used

AZGF	Arizona Game and Fish Department
BNT	Brown trout (*Salmo trutta*)
GCMRC	Grand Canyon Monitoring & Research Center, U.S. Geological Survey
HBC	Humpback chub (*Gila cypha*)
HFE	High-flow experiment
LCR	Little Colorado River
NPS	National Park Service, Department of the Interior
PBR	Paria to Badger reach, Colorado River
RBT	Rainbow trout (*Onchorhynchus mykiss*)
Reclamation	Bureau of Reclamation, Department of the Interior
RM	River mile (location along the Colorado River, relative to Lees Ferry)
ROD	1996 Record of Decision

Hybrid Portfolio A: *No Action Alternative (Single strategies: 1, 6).* Doing nothing is an action that has consequences. In this 'no action' portfolio, RBT are not removed in the mainstem, ROD flow regimes are maintained, and the ongoing trout reduction program at Bright Angel Creek (which targets BNT but removes RBT as well) continues as initiated by NPS. No efforts to reduce RBT migration or directly enhance HBC populations are undertaken. The intent of this portfolio is to provide a default for comparison to other portfolios, which would be justified if RBT do not limit HBC recovery. Trout removal at Bright Angel Creek is conducted by NPS or their contractors. The underlying hypotheses are that the HBC population at LCR is not limited by RBT abundance, although BNT do limit HBC.

Hybrid Portfolio B: *Status Quo (Single strategies: 2, 6).* This portfolio represents the removal of RBT at LCR that had been conducted during the experimental period (2003–06) and one additional time in spring 2009. These actions involve multiple trips per year and multiple depletion passes per trip. The magnitude, and therefore effort and cost, of the removal depends on abundance in LCR relative to the abundance target, which is 600 to 1,200 RBT in the LCR confluence reach based on 10–20 percent of 2003 RBT abundance. Removal of RBT is followed by euthanasia and use for fertilizer. Removal of BNT is by weir and electrofishing during October and January, and BNT are prepared for human consumption. Actions aimed at RBT in the main channel of the Colorado River are conducted by Reclamation, or AZGF (as contractor to GCMRC) and those actions aimed at BNT are conducted by NPS or their contractors. The underlying hypotheses are that RBT and BNT limit HBC and that movement of RBT from Lees Ferry to LCR cannot be effectively reduced or eliminated, particularly when RBT production is increased by repeated HFEs.

Hybrid Portfolios C_1, C_2, C_3, C_4, and C_5: *Culturally sensitive removal at LCR (Single strategies: 3, 6).* These portfolios involve removal of RBT in the LCR reach, but include options for the method of capture and beneficial use that could meet tribal concerns. Trout (and possibly HBC) population size at the LCR is used as a trigger for removal. The method of capture is electrofishing. Options for beneficial use include euthanasia and preservation for human consumption (C_1), euthanasia and freezing for animal consumption (C_2), or live removal and transport for release outside of the Colorado River system (C_3, C_4, and C_5; these three differ in the amount and the method of live removal, see table 3). Actions aimed at RBT in the main channel of the Colorado River are conducted by Reclamation or AZGF (as contractor to GCMRC) and those actions aimed at BNT are conducted by NPS or their contractors. The underlying hypotheses are that RBT and BNT limit HBC and that movement of RBT from Lees Ferry to LCR cannot be effectively reduced, particularly when RBT production is increased by repeated HFEs.

Hybrid Portfolios D_1, D_2, and D_3: *Removal curtain (Single strategies: 3, 5, and 6).* These portfolios combines a short-term strategy of removing RBT at the LCR to reduce the existing threat with a long-term strategy of removing RBT in the PBR to reduce or eliminate movement from Lees Ferry to LCR (that is, the creation of a "curtain" that blocks downstream movement by removing RBT in the PBR). The removal at LCR is triggered in the same way as Portfolio C, but is expected to be needed only about a third as often. The magnitude of removal at PBR is based on either a fixed effort applied annually or an undefined trigger. The three versions of D differ in the method of removal and the beneficial use: D_1 includes lethal removal at both LCR and PBR; D_2 includes lethal removal at LCR, but live removal at PBR; and D_3 includes live removal at both LCR (via helicopter) and PBR. BNT removal is conducted in Bright Angel Creek as described in Portfolio A. Actions aimed at RBT in the main channel of the Colorado River are conducted by Reclamation, or AZGF (as contractor to GCMRC) and those actions aimed at BNT are conducted by NPS or their contractors. The underlying hypotheses are that RBT and BNT limit HBC, which can be alleviated by reducing or eliminating movement from the Lees Ferry tailwaters reach (for RBT). Also, movement of RBT from Lees Ferry to LCR can be effectively reduced or eliminated through removal, but not through flow or sediment augmentation.

Hybrid Portfolio E: *Sediment curtain (Single strategies: 3b, 5e, 6, 13).* This portfolio combines a short-term strategy of removing RBT at LCR and PBR to reduce the extant threat with a long-term strategy of sediment augmentation to reduce or eliminate movement from Lees Ferry to LCR. The magnitude of short-term removal is similar to Portfolio B, but the magnitude of removal at PBR is based on either a fixed effort applied annually or an undefined trigger. Options for method of capture and beneficial use are similar to Portfolio C_2. BNT removal is conducted as described in Portfolio A. Sediment is augmented at Paria through construction of a sediment pipeline from above Glen Canyon Dam. Actions aimed at RBT in the main channel of the Colorado River are conducted by Reclamation, or AZGF (as contractor to GCMRC) and those actions aimed at BNT are conducted by NPS or their contractors. The underlying hypotheses are that RBT and BNT limit HBC, which can be alleviated by reducing or eliminating movement from Lees Ferry (for RBT). Also, movement of RBT from Lees Ferry to LCR can be effectively reduced or eliminated through sediment augmentation in the long term (see Randle and others 2007).

Hybrid Portfolio F: *Stranding flow (Single strategies: 6, 11).* This portfolio varies flow to strand 0-age trout and reduce juvenile survival and recruitment of RBT in the Lees Ferry tailwaters reach. The intent is to reduce or eliminate movement of RBT from Lees Ferry to the LCR reach. High steady flows (20,000 cubic feet per second [ft^3/s]; 17,500 ft^3/s if maintenance limitations constrain operations) are maintained for 2 to 4 days followed by rapid decline to 2,500–5,000 ft^3/s for 12 hours to 1 day. These flows are implemented during May 1–August 1, and repeated twice a month (for six cycles total). BNT removal is conducted in Bright Angel Creek as described in Portfolio A. Flow is managed by Reclamation. The underlying hypotheses are that HBC are limited by RBT and that the threat can be reduced or eliminated effectively by stranding flows.

Hybrid Portfolio F': *Stranding flow with stocking of triploid male trout (Single strategies: 6, 11, 16)*. This portfolio is identical to Portfolio F, with the addition of trout stocking at Lees Ferry to offset reductions in the trout population. AZGF manages stocking operations. The underlying hypotheses are the HBC are limited by RBT and that the threat can be reduced by stranding flows; addition of stocked trout is needed to meet the objectives of the recreational angling community.

Hybrid Portfolio G: *Stranding flow with augmentation (Single strategies: 5e, 6, 11)*. This portfolio uses short-term removal from the PBR and variation in flow to strand 0-age trout to reduce juvenile survival and recruitment of RBT. The intent is to reduce or eliminate movement of RBT from Lees Ferry to LCR reach initially through removal at PBR, but in the long run through flow variation. High steady flows (20,000 ft^3/s; 17,500 ft^3/s if maintenance limitations constrain operations) are maintained for 2 to 4 days followed by rapid decline to 2,500–5,000 ft^3/s for 12 hours to 1 day. These flows are implemented during May 1–August 1, and repeated twice a month (for six cycles total). The magnitude of removal at PBR is based on either a fixed effort applied annually or an undefined trigger. Options for method of capture and beneficial use are similar to Portfolio C$_2$. BNT removal is conducted in Bright Angel Creek as described in Portfolio A. Flow is managed by Reclamation. Removal is conducted by Reclamation or AZGF (as contractor to GCMRC) and NPS or their contractors. The underlying hypotheses are that HBC are limited by RBT and that the threat can be reduced by stranding flows, but initially removal at PBR is needed to reduce or eliminate the threat in the short term.

Hybrid Portfolio G': *Stranding flow with augmentation and stocking of triploid male trout (Single strategies: 5e, 6, 11, 16)*. This portfolio is similar to Portfolio G, but with the addition of trout stocking for the same reasons as in Porfolio F'.

Hybrid Portfolio H: *Stranding flow with assurances (Single strategies: 3b, 6, 11)*. This portfolio uses short-term removal at LCR reach and variation in flow to strand 0-age trout to reduce juvenile survival and recruitment of RBT. The intent is to reduce or eliminate movement of RBT from Lees Ferry to LCR, with the removal of RBT from LCR as needed, especially in the short term. The magnitude of short-term removal is similar to Portfolio B. Options for method of capture and beneficial use are similar to Portfolio C$_2$. High steady flows (20,000 ft^3/s; 17,500 ft^3/s if maintenance limitations constrain operations) are maintained for 2 to 4 days followed by rapid decline to 2,500–5,000 ft^3/s for 12 hours to 1 day. These flows are implemented during May 1–August 1, and repeated twice a month (for six cycles total). BNT removal is conducted in Bright Angel Creek as described in Portfolio A. Flow is managed by Reclamation. Removal is conducted by Reclamation or AZGF (as contractor to GCMRC) and NPS or their contractors. The underlying hypotheses are the HBC are limited by RBT and that the threat can be reduced by stranding flows, but removal at LCR is needed to eliminate the threat, at least initially.

Hybrid Portfolio H': *Stranding flow with assurances with stocking of triploid male trout (Single strategies: 3b, 6, 11, 16)*. This portfolio is similar to Portfolio H, but with the addition of trout stocking for the same reasons as in Porfolio F'.

Hybrid Portfolio I: *Dewater redds with assurances (Single strategies: 5e, 6, 9)*. This portfolio uses removal from the PBR and variation in flow to dewater redds and reduce juvenile survival and recruitment of RBT. The intent is to reduce or eliminate movement of RBT from Lees Ferry to LCR, initially through removal at PBR, but in the long-run through dewatering redds. Up to 20,000 ft^3/s maximum daily flow for 13 days (minimum daily flow doesn't matter). On day 14, drop flow to 2,500–

5,000 ft^3/s between 8 am–1 pm, then resume normal ROD operations. These flows are implemented during February 1–April 30. The magnitude of removal at PBR is based on either a fixed effort applied annually or an undefined trigger. Options for method of capture and beneficial use are similar to Portfolio C$_2$. BNT removal is conducted in Bright Angel Creek as described in Portfolio A. Flow is managed by Reclamation. The underlying hypotheses are that HBC are limited by RBT and that the threat can be reduced by flows to dewater redds, but removal at PBR is needed to remove the compensatory effect (enhanced survival of young fish that emerge from eggs that are not killed through dewatering) and reduce or eliminate the threat to HBC.

Hybrid Portfolios J$_1$ and J$_2$: *Kitchen Sink I and II (Single strategies: 3, 5, 6, 7, 8, 9, 10, 11).* These portfolios combine a wide variety of flow and non-flow actions simultaneously. The intent is to do everything conceivable to reduce trout production in the Lees Ferry tailwaters reach, reduce emigration to the LCR reach, reduce predation of HBC, and improve recruitment of HBC. Removal magnitude and methods are similar to Portfolio D. The two versions of the portfolio differ in the removal method, with J$_1$ using lethal methods (3b, 5e) and J$_2$ using live removal methods (3e, 5h). Flow methods are similar to Portfolios E, F, G, and H. BNT removal is conducted in Bright Angel Creek as described in Portfolio A. Flow is managed by Reclamation. Removal is conducted by Reclamation or AZGF (as contractor to GCMRC) and NPS or their contractors. The underlying hypotheses are that HBC are threatened by RBT at the LCR to some degree, movement of RBT to LCR can be managed partially through flow and fishery regulations to reduce or eliminate threat at LCR.

> Hybrid Portfolios J1' and J2': *Kitchen Sink I and II with stocking of triploid male trout (Single strategies: 3, 5, 6, 7, 8, 9, 10, 11, 16).* These strategies are similar to J1 and J2, but with the addition of stocking of triploid trout, for the same reasons and by the same methods as described in Portfolio F'. AZGF would manage stocking operations.

Hybrid Portfolio K: *Zuni-Hopi-NPS strategy (Single strategies: 5h, 6, 9, 17).* This portfolio combines live removal of RBT in PBR, BNT removal at Bright Angel, stranding (redd dewatering) flows, and expanded harvest of trout at Lees Ferry. The intent of the portfolio is to limit downstream emigration, enhance HBC population at LCR and avoid unnecessary taking of life. The magnitude of removal at PBR is based on a fixed effort applied annually; removal method is live removal with beneficial use. Stranding flows focus on dewatering redds. BNT removal is conducted in Bright Angel Creek as described in Portfolio A. Harvest in the Lees Ferry tailwaters reach is expanded to reduce population size. Flow is managed by Reclamation. Removal is conducted by Reclamation or AZGF (as contractor to GCMRC) and NPS or their contractors. AZGF manages the fishery at Lees Ferry. The underlying hypotheses are that HBC are threatened by RBT at the LCR to some degree, movement of RBT to the LCR can be managed partially through flow and fishery regulations to reduce or eliminate threat at the LCR

Hybrid Portfolio L: *Strategy K plus headstarting and barrier (Single strategies: 5h, 6, 9, 15, 17, 18).* This portfolio combines live removal of RBT in PBR, BNT removal at Bright Angel, stranding (redd dewatering flows), expanded harvest of trout at Lees Ferry, a headstarting program for HBC, and barriers to downstream emigration. The intent of the portfolio is to limit downstream emigration, enhance HBC population at the LCR and avoid unnecessary taking of life. The magnitude of removal at PBR is based on a fixed effort applied annually; removal method is live removal with beneficial use. Redd dewatering flows are employed. BNT removal is conducted in Bright Angel Creek as described in Portfolio A. Harvest at Lees Ferry is expanded to reduce population size. The methods for headstarting HBC are undetermined. The barrier could be fine-sediment augmentation, similar to Portfolio E, or electrical, sound, or floating net, but not a constructed barrier. Flow is managed by Reclamation. Removal is conducted by Reclamation or AZGF (as contractor to GCMRC) and NPS or their contractors. AZGF manages the fishery at Lees Ferry. The lead on HBC culture is undetermined. The lead on barrier development is undetermined. The underlying hypotheses are that (1) HBC are threatened by RBT at LCR to some degree and (2) movement of RBT to LCR can be managed partially through flow and fishery regulations, but that additional measures (barrier and headstarting) will be needed to reduce or eliminate threat at LCR.

Hybrid Portfolio M: *Selective-sacrifice and strand portfolio (Single strategies: 5j, 6, 9 with trigger).* This portfolio combines removal of RBT in PBR based on an abundance trigger at Lees Ferry, beneficial use of removed fish, BNT removal in Bright Angel, and stranding flows to dewater redds. The intent of the portfolio is to limit downstream emigration, enhance HBC population at LCR, minimize need for removal, and incorporate beneficial use of removed fish. The magnitude of removal at PBR is based on either a fixed effort applied annually or an undefined trigger. Options for method of capture and beneficial use are similar to Portfolio C. BNT removal is conducted in Bright Angel Creek as described in Portfolio A. Flows are similar to Portfolio I. Flow is managed by Reclamation. Removal is conducted by Reclamation or AZGF (as contractor to GCMRC) and NPS or their contractors. The underlying hypotheses are that HBC are threatened by RBT at LCR to some degree, movement of RBT to LCR can be managed partially through flow, but some removal will be necessary in the PBR to reduce or eliminate the threat at LCR.

Hybrid Portfolio N: *BNT expanded removal (Single strategies: 1, 3b, 6, 7, 8).* This portfolio combines no action on RBT with an expanded effort to remove BNT from multiple tributaries in addition to Bright Angel Creek and to incorporate BNT removal as a standard operating procedure in fish monitoring activities. The intent of the portfolio is to enhance the HBC population at the LCR by eliminating BNT from the system to the degree possible. BNT removal is conducted in Bright Angel Creek as described in Portfolio A. BNT are also removed in multiple tributaries and during monitoring activities using weir and electrofishing. Removal is conducted by Reclamation or AZGF (as contractor to GCMRC) and NPS or their contractors. The underlying hypotheses are that HBC are threatened by BNT at LCR and extirpation of BNT from the system is needed to reduce or eliminate the threat at LCR.

Hybrid Portfolio O: *Expanded sediment curtain (Single strategies: 3b, 5e, 6, 13, 14).* This portfolio combines short-term removal of RBT at LCR to reduce the extant threat with long-term management to reduce movement of RBT to LCR using fine-sediment augmentation (via pipeline from upstream sources in Lake Powell; see Randle and others 2007). The intent of the portfolio is to enhance HBC at LCR by reducing RBT by short-term removal followed by long term fine-sediment augmentation. The portfolio is similar to Portfolio E, but sediment is augmented at an upstream point in the Lees Ferry tailwaters reach (presumably, to attenuate dramatic increases in primary production following HFEs) as well as at the Paria River confluence. The magnitude of removal is similar to Portfolio B, but magnitude of removal at PBR is based on either a fixed effort applied annually or an undefined trigger. Options for method of capture and beneficial use are similar to Portfolio C_2. BNT removal is conducted in Bright Angel Creek as described in Portfolio A. Actions are conducted by Reclamation or AZGF (as contractor to GCMRC) and NPS or their contractors. The underlying hypotheses are that HBC are threatened by RBT at LCR, flow or fishery management at Lees Ferry is not effective, and fine-sediment augmentation at Lees Ferry and Paria will be effective methods to reduce or eliminate the threat at LCR.

Reference Cited

Randle, T.J., Lyons, J.K., Christensen, R.J., and Stephen, R.D., 2007, Colorado River ecosystem sediment augmentation appraisal engineering report, Bureau of Reclamation, 71 p.